got milk?

Prima Publishing

the book

jeff manning

Prima Publishing and colophon are registered trademarks of Prima Communications, Inc.

Library of Congress Cataloging-in-Publication Data
Manning, Jeff.
    Got milk? : the book / Jeff Manning.
      p. cm.
      Includes index.
      ISBN 0-7615-1801-0
      1. Advertising—Milk. 2. Milk trade—United States. I. Title.
    HF6161.M53M36 1999
    659.1'96371'0973—dc21   99-30813
                                          CIP

99 00 01 GG 10 9 8 7 6 5 4 3 2 1
Printed in the United States of America

How to Order
Single copies may be ordered from Prima Publishing, P.O. Box 1260BK, Rocklin, CA 95677; telephone (916) 632-4400. Quantity discounts are also available. On your letterhead, include information concerning the intended use of the books and the number of books you wish to purchase.

Visit us online at www.primalifestyles.com
or www.gotmilk.com

To my family, my board, and my agency

          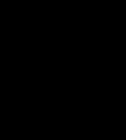  

contents

Introduction

Isolation. Desperation. Torture. What strange origins for an advertising campaign, and for a book. Yet these were the "godparents" of GOT MILK?

You probably have your favorite GOT MILK? ads. The weird history buff, mouth crammed with peanut butter, who loses $10,000 because he runs out of milk and therefore can't say "Aaron Burr." Or perhaps the priest who, having stuffed his face with devil's food cake, goes ballistic because the vending machine won't give up his milk. My vote goes to the one in which a clearly nasty guy gets flattened by a truck. With an angelic tour guide and a limitless supply of discus-size cookies, he thinks he's landed in heaven. But without milk, he realizes he's toasting a long way to the south.

What bonds together these and the other 30 or so GOT MILK? spots? Why do they seem to touch us so?

Regardless of our age, gender, or slot in society, why do we not only giggle, but often choke with laughter?

The answer lies in an odd place: a place of deprivation versus abundance. A place where regular people, with their compulsions and obsessions, are reminded just how horrible the world would be without milk. No milk for their cereal or with their cake or chocolate chip cookies. No milk for their kids or their cats. Can you imagine pouring Snapple on your Cheerios or dunking your Oreos in iced tea? We love GOT MILK? for one simple reason: it's true. Running out of milk, especially with a mouthful of food, is one big pain in the proverbial butt.

What kind of people, what kind of tormented minds, came up with GOT MILK? Surprisingly, they aren't all that weird. Sure, one guy has a ponytail and another a diluted English accent, but they're relatively normal and, under most circumstances, harmless. It's just that they view the world through a somewhat different lens—a lens that spots a small indiscretion, such as running out of milk, and magnifies it into a capital offense.

Another GOT MILK? question to ponder is whether these two words (and the cult they spawned) were the result of long, rigorous hours of careful calculation or simply the offspring of dumb luck? The truth is a little of both. Research and the linear thought that trails it were certainly a factor. Someone had to study the market for milk and try to figure out why consumption was going down the toilet. But logic alone could not have conceived GOT MILK? nor pro-

duced the resulting laughter. It needed a touch of brilliance and a fair-sized dose of luck. No one set out to make GOT MILK? part of America's pop culture and vernacular. We hoped to do some really good advertising and got a whole lot more.

The GOT MILK? campaign has touched virtually every person in this country. From the senior citizen with his bowl of Grapenuts. To the teenage boy chugging straight from the carton. To the infant who will tear down the house for her bottle. The story of GOT MILK? will make you smile because it's a true story. You, the American public, gobbled GOT MILK? up and kept coming back for more.

Logic alone could not have conceived got milk? nor produced the resulting laughter.

chapter 1

The World Before got milk?

How could two commercials—one about a duel and one about a lying husband—change the course of American advertising? And how could two words and a question mark leapfrog logic to become a part of our pop culture and vernacular? It was October 1993, and the answers lie in the advertising.

Aaron Burr The commercial opens on a studio apartment set in what looks to be a deserted factory. Classical music plays softly. The camera pans across several antique collections to reveal a strange-looking young man methodically spreading peanut butter on bread with a carving knife. We cut to *Hamilton's Memoirs,* then a painting of Alexander Hamilton. We drift back to the man who is folding and wedging a peanut butter sandwich into his mouth. The music ends and the radio DJ announces, "That was the Vienna Wood Dance in B, one of my all-time favorites. And now, that random call with today's $10,000 question . . . who shot Alexander Hamilton in that famous duel?"

We see two antique guns, a statue of Hamilton, a portrait of Aaron Burr, and the famous bullet in a glass case. The man, mouth crammed with peanut butter, sits in front of his phone and a carton of milk. The phone rings. The man snatches up the receiver and says, "Hewo." The DJ asks, "For $10,000, who shot—" Our hero cuts him off to answer, "Aaaawon Buuuhh." The DJ can't understand him. The man screams "Aaaawon Buuuhh" and reaches for the milk carton. He pours, but gets only a few drops. The DJ says, "I'm afraid your time is almost up." Another garbled "Aaaawon Buuuhh." The DJ says, "I'm sorry. Maybe next time."

Pathetically, to the sound of the dial tone, the man mumbles, "Aaaawon Buuuhh." The screen goes black and, for the first of many, many times, up pop the words "GOT MILK?"

Couple The scene opens on a husband sleepily entering a dark kitchen, his wife sitting at the table, staring into space. In front of her is a bowl of Honey Nut Cheerios, a spoon, and a carton of milk. He asks innocently, "What's the matter? Couldn't you sleep?" She replies, "Did you think I wouldn't find out?" Taken aback, he grabs a banana and asks, "Is this about the ring I gave you?" Without waiting for an answer, he goes on, "Listen . . . a cubic zirconia looks just like a real diamond."

The wife looks perplexed and studies her engagement ring. He sits down across from her and tries another question: "Is this about my time in prison?" His wife looks up in disbelief, picks up the empty carton, and reveals what she's been talking about all along: "You drank the last of the milk." We cut back to the husband who looks at once befuddled and exposed. He only manages a weak smile before the screen goes black and "GOT MILK?" appears.

Before these commercials launched the GOT MILK? campaign in October 1993, the world had fewer giggles and far less intelligent advertising. Sure, there were a few funny commercials and some smart advertisers, but campaigns that were at once relevant, humorous, and sustainable were singularly lacking. GOT MILK? filled that gap and stood up to years, not just months, of exposure. It was a campaign that people actually sought out, talked about, and could recall with almost surreal accuracy.

For the milk industry, the decades leading up to GOT MILK? were sad, and more than a little sobering. Milk, had once dominated the beverage business. It certainly had occupied center stage in American refrigerators. Milk was fresh, natural, readily available, and affordable. It was pure, wholesome, and as close to a patriotic drink as one could get. Milk was part of the bacon and eggs breakfast, the ham and cheese lunch, the meat and potatoes dinner. People "back then" ate most of their food as meals and most of their meals at home. Milk's competition was limited to orange juice and tap water. Local milk brands were powerful forces, and consumers treated them as part of their families.

But, like the beef and egg industries, the milk industry had become complacent, put their business on autopilot, and begun to glide. Focused squarely on the supply side, they had failed to take notice of monumental changes in

consumer tastes and eating habits. Families were eating out more often, women were working outside the home in unprecedented numbers, and people were getting considerably more experimental in their beverage tastes. As a result, far fewer family meals were being eaten around the kitchen table, and milk was one of the casualties. Milk was in desperate need of resurrection.

The milk industry had also ignored two little companies named Coca-Cola and McDonald's. Coca-Cola was moving toward its primary mission: putting a Coke within 30 feet of every human on earth. Soft drink vending machines were sprouting like mold and infiltrating every corner of our lives, including our schools. Meanwhile, McDonald's had launched the fast-food wars, diverting hundreds of millions of meals from the kitchen counter to the restaurant counter. And people showed little inclination to drink milk while wolfing down french fries, munching on fried chicken, or stuffing their gullets with pizza.

Other competitive assaults that didn't bode well for milk followed. "New Age" beverages, isotonics (or sports drinks), and bottled waters started to flex their marketing muscle. Refrigerators, long the domain of milk and juice, were being stocked with multiple flavors of Snapple. Teenage boys, the bottomless pits of the beverage industry, were downing massive quantities of swamp-green Gatorade. And women were carrying Evian bottles like modern gunslingers. The cola wars were in full swing, with Coke and Pepsi spending sinful amounts of money on advertising and promotion. The competition for "share of mouth" was heating up, and milk, along with tap water, was losing.

"Good for You" Not Necessarily Good for Business

On the milk marketing front, decades of "good for you" advertising were having little effect on sales or consumption. Milk commercials from around the world demonstrated that it didn't matter if one was in the United Kingdom or the United States, Austria or Australia, the only thing the milk industry had to say was "It's good for you." The other universal denominator in advertising was the presence of cows. The dairy industry obviously adored everything bovine.

The problem, at least in the United States, was that 92 percent of the public already believed that milk was good for them. And they sure knew that milk didn't come from

chickens. Milk consumption in the 1980s and early 1990s was going down the proverbial toilet, dropping at an ever faster rate. Milk was being outpackaged, outspent, and outflanked. Consumers didn't hate milk. They simply had shifted gears and left it behind.

What was the milk industry doing in the face of this decline? Not much more than filling cartons. Sure, there

got milk? GETS A MUSTACHE

The dairy industry goes out of its way to confuse people. It starts by having several national milk boards and an uncountable number of regional, state, and local groups.

Just in case someone spends the time to figure these out, the industry gives every organization an acronym.

Here's a mere sample: DMI, DI, NDB, UDIA, IDFA, DFA, CMAB, and CMPB (that's us). There is also a group called MilkPEP, who are the folks that created and fund the milk mustache campaign, which started running ads in January 1995. Needless to say, people—regular, normal, nondairy-industry people—get the GOT MILK? and Milk Mustache campaigns mixed up.

In truth, we're closely related. Both campaigns are funded by milk processors—the Milk Mustache program on the national level, and GOT MILK? in California. My organization, the California Milk Processor Board, licenses the GOT MILK? trademark and advertising to MilkPEP, which is why the phrase appears in print ads below all those wonderful celebrities sporting milk mustaches.

Are the Milk Mustache and GOT MILK? campaigns compatible? Do the health and nutrition messages embedded in the Milk Mustache ads work for or against milk deprivation, our strategic superstructure? Do consumers even notice that there are two campaigns? Or is it all just milk advertising? Good questions.

The reality is that consumers don't give a twit about who sponsors what. They either like the ads, find them memorable and compelling, or they don't. They don't know or care that the Milk Mustache and GOT MILK? campaigns were created by different ad agencies and funded by different dairy groups. Research, observation, and common sense indicate that people are attracted and attached to the merged campaigns. Kids collect posters with celebrities, with chocolate chip cookies, and with Cookie Monster (one of our promotion partners). They all say "GOT MILK?", and they all work to make milk more competitive.

were generic milk campaigns, including the memorable "Does A Body Good," which proposed that drinking milk would make kids grow taller and stronger. But milk's profile and image were rapidly eroding. The industry desperately needed an injection of fresh and provocative thinking.

In 1991, well aware of the plight of their product, milk processors from around the country (under the guidance of the International Dairy Food Association [IDFA]) tried to create a huge generic advertising campaign. (Milk processors are the companies who convert raw milk into the stuff we buy at the store.) Even before getting the program funded, the IDFA invited advertising agencies to "pitch" the milk account. Two agencies battled it out. I happened to work for the loser. Although we didn't get the account, we did develop an interesting concept: selling milk by associating it with a select list of foods, eating occasions, and celebrities. The campaign, presented in very rough form, was based on the line: "MILK & _____."

MILK & COOKIES. MILK & CEREAL. MILK & MOM. MILK & MADONNA. MILK & MONDAY NIGHT FOOTBALL.

The new milk campaign didn't get off the ground. The industry just wasn't ready for a $100 million program. The winning agency, Bozell Worldwide, wisely adopted a long-term view of the account and continued to work on this potentially huge piece of business. (When

the national program was finally funded, a year after GOT MILK? was launched, it became the now famous Milk Mustache campaign.) As for me, the idea of selling milk and its complementary foods settled in a crevice of my mind.

Moving Beyond Cows and Calcium

In 1993, California milk processors, in the form of the California Milk Processor Board (CMPB), decided to take charge of their own marketing destiny. They were acutely

aware of the free fall in milk consumption. They weren't sure they wanted a national campaign, but they sure wanted one within the borders of their state. The nine board members represented all California milk processors. The board was headed by Dick Walrack, who hails from Montana and is, in his own words, an "operations guy." He knows how to build and run a dairy plant, one that can process and package millions of gallons of milk per week. He also knows how to "make stuff happen." (In addition to these talents, Dick gained my unbounded respect when I learned that he and his wife Kay drove from Bozeman, Montana, to Los Angeles, California, in a 1950s station wagon with five kids under the age of ten.)

Dick and I came at milk marketing in the same way: create great advertising and sell more milk. Succeed and the advertising program continues. Fail and it dies. With the board's support, I became CMPB's first employee. My immediate charge was to hire the best advertising agency in the country.

got milk?

chapter 2

The Pitch

The ad campaign for the California Milk Processor Board was going to be a brand new account for some lucky agency. We were fresh meat.

Usually, advertising agencies battle each other for an existing piece of the pie. In other words, clients often jump ship and look

got milk?

for new ad agencies. That doesn't mean the agency isn't doing good work. The dissatisfaction could come from sagging sales, disgruntled franchisers, or new management. But the result is the same: a review of advertising agencies, which is a polite way of saying "shopping around." The client has the none-too-pleasant task of informing his current agency of the review. He then calls other agencies and invites them to "pitch" the business or, if he's trying to keep it low key, to "just talk."

A client reviewing his advertising agency is a bit like a husband coming home and saying, oh so sweetly, to his wife, "Don't take this personally—you still mean the world to me. But I'm going to sleep with several other women over the next month or so. Women who say they'll do absolutely anything for me, things you would never do. To be fair, I also want to bed you a few times. And when I have more perspective on what I want, I'll let you know who wins. By the way, if this dating thing isn't okay with you, you can always divorce me. No hard feelings." Is this an exaggeration? Not really. While many agency reviews are conducted in a highly professional manner, in the end, clients make their agency decisions on the basis of virtual one-nighters.

In our case, there was no past, no incumbent, no existing campaign. In fact, in June 1993, there wasn't even an office or letterhead. Only this ex-agency guy in Berkeley (me) with a budget of around $25 million. Prior to my being hired, the board had initiated the ad agency review using the services of a consultant. I chose to let the consultant go for two reasons. One, I had spent 25 years on the agency side, the last 10 as a director of new business. While I clearly had shortcomings, evaluating an agency wasn't one of them. Two, since my rear end was going to be on the line for

This experience solidified for me one of the underlying principles of my business life: go for content and screw the fluff.

results, it was imperative that the agency be compatible with my vision and style. The board agreed, and the consultant disappeared.

At the end of my first day on the job, I carried home 22 proposals from agencies small to monolithic. After a few hours of reading, I felt as if someone had spiked my Diet Coke with novocaine. I was numb with adjectives and imperatives. It literally hurt to look at another biography or organization chart. Ten of the proposals were virtually interchangeable. One of these particularly struck me in its lack of definition and distinction. The depressing yet humorous fact was that I had written it myself, on behalf of the agency for which I worked at the time. I had labored for weeks over its creation, giving it every bit of persuasiveness in me—and it had turned out to be a bundle of hype. My alma mater didn't make the cut.

Somewhere around 2 A.M., I had whittled the list down to four agencies, based almost entirely on the quality of their ideas for other clients. All those words, all those charts, all those leather binders didn't mean squat. This experience solidified for me one of the underlying principles of my business life: go for content and screw the fluff. Good people will recognize good ideas and good work. If they don't, well, you probably don't want to work with them.

One of the four agencies was a small, obscure but emerging shop called Goodby, Berlin & Silverstein (now Goodby, Silverstein & Partners). Despite

The advertising community is openly incestuous. Peers become clients. Competitors become clients. Ex-clients become clients. And worst of all, fired employees become clients.

sounding more like a law firm than a creative resource, they had done some irreverent, provocative work, mostly for local West Coast clients. I had worked briefly with two of the three principals—Jeff Goodby and Rich Silverstein. To complicate matters, Rich's wife had once worked for me. (The advertising community is openly incestuous. Peers become clients. Competitors become clients. Ex-clients become clients. And worst of all, fired employees become clients.) The three other agencies made for an interesting mix. Included was the largest agency in San Francisco, the guru of San Francisco advertising, Hal Riney & Partners, as well as a feisty little shop known for its intensely competitive work.

Once the finalists in the milk pitch (a word that completely fails to connote the levels of anxiety and competition involved) were chosen, I visited each agency to get a sense of both the people and the place and to provide insight into what my board and I were seeking. These warm-up meetings were like verbal foreplay. Most of the agencies tried to portray themselves the way they thought we wanted them to be: wildly creative, highly disciplined, just regular guys, or global players in the advertising industry.

This chameleon effect is actually quite impressive. For a major financial service prospect (for example, American Express or Charles Schwab), a group of agency folks will wear designer suits and babble about multifactor analyses. The next day, these same people are sockless, resemble a denim ad, and purr softly about unearthing creative insights. For our meetings, most of the agency people wore their "sincere suits and ties," while I showed up in Gap attire.

Force-Feeding a Point of View

The key to the eventual development of GOT MILK? was that each agency was given (force-fed) my point of view on how to market milk. In brief, I noted that people don't spontaneously say, "Damn, I need a big glass of milk now." Rather, they make the decision to have some Oreos, build a peanut butter and jelly sandwich, or pour a bowl of Cheerios. Only after they've made the food decision do they then scan the refrigerator for the right beverage.

With these foods, that beverage has got to be milk. So I gave the four finalists the Manning "Food & Milk" strategy. (Actually, it should have been called the Dudwick strategy. Ken Dudwick, a man I worked with decades ago, is one of the people who gave life to GOT MILK? It was Ken, years before Jeff Goodby uttered the magic words "GOT MILK?," who gave me the idea of selling milk by reminding people of its indelible link to food.)

It was tough not to favor the folks from Goodby. They were thoughtful, confident, likable, and humble. While their creative work was clearly superlative, they didn't pound their chests and refer to the dozens of awards they had won. Rather, they reflected on how they went about solving problems for their clients and how

In my life as an ad man, I had seen grown men and women, most of whom had superb vocabularies, screaming at each other over the use of the descriptor "large" versus "significant."

they might approach the milk business. But what was most memorable about the hours I spent at Goodby was that they asked a series of probing, provocative questions. And then they listened to the answers. This was in blinding contrast to some other agency people, who spoke almost exclusively in first-person singular and rarely allowed me to get my two-and-a-half cents in. Giving the agencies two weeks to prepare final presentations, I outlined what I expected (an intelligent, no-holds-barred discussion of how to sell more milk) and said I was available to answer any and all questions.

A Slice of Chaos

I knew from my own experience in advertising that the four agencies, having made the finals, would now be starting to "taste blood." The weeks leading up to a presentation require outrageously long days, sometimes all-nighters, on the part of the agency's creative team. The number of changes made in the final 24 hours can reach ludicrous proportions. In my life as an ad man, I had seen grown men and women, most of whom had superb vocabularies, screaming at each other over the use of the descriptor "large" versus "significant."

Each agency designated a small conference room as the "Milk War Room." It was filled with graphs and charts, scraps of paper, drawings, and idea fragments taped to the walls, floor, and ceiling. Dozens of videotapes were strewn about. As ad agencies are fundamentally paranoid, no one except people working on the new pitch was allowed in the war room. By the time of the final

presentation, the room was a mosaic of greasy pizza boxes, discarded Starbucks cups, and crumpled Diet Coke cans. And, of course, lots of pictures of ice-cold milk.

According to Jeff Goodby, while their war room was equally cluttered and disgusting, it was markedly different in one way. There were pictures of cookies and

cereal and peanut butter, but no milk. No glistening glasses of the white stuff, no nutrition charts, no healthy glowing faces, and no famous people guzzling milk. Just some videotapes of people with cookies in their mouths mumbling about how they were about to die without milk.

For some agencies, the last night before a presentation is a slice of chaos. Decisions are made one of three ways. Somebody is the boss, and he or she says, "Enough of this crap. We're going with option #2. I'm going to sleep, you're not. See you at 7 A.M." Or, if the president or CEO

has read the most recent book on consensus management, the scenario is more like: "How do you really feel, Chuck? Are you strongly behind that idea, Susan? Michael, your body language suggests that you have something to share." This approach proves lethal. It tears the heart out of the group, escalates stress levels, and leads to Jell-O-like presentations. Lastly, one time in a million, almost everybody agrees on what to recommend, and they all hit the sack early.

At Goodby, Berlin & Silverstein, the night before the milk pitch wasn't all that crazy. They were good presenters. They had a terrific reel of commercials. They had done some enlightening, provocative research. And they had two standard presentation boards. One read "Milk Deprivation," and the other, "GOT MILK?"

Ironically, the tag line that launched an advertising tour de force arrived as an almost offhanded remark by Jeff Goodby. Asked by an underling for a heading to a new presentation board, Jeff, who was a man in a hurry, considered the idea of running out of milk only for a moment before tossing out the phrase "GOT MILK?" The person asked earnestly if he didn't mean, "Do you have any milk?" Jeff replied that it was too long and this was advertising, not a class in grammar. Make it "GOT MILK?" Without realizing the brilliance of what he had just uttered, Jeff returned to what he had been working on before the interruption.

A couple
of the agencies
worked hard
to eliminate
themselves.

The Final Pitch

That brilliant gem was first displayed in an unremarkable conference room in Southern California, a room with all the warmth and humanity of a biotech lab. Hard lighting. Faulty equipment. Lukewarm coffee. And in the room next door, a swarm of over-amplified car salesmen. Ahead of us lay four presentations and one long day. Each ad agency had two hours to pitch a nice little $25 million piece of business.

On our side of the table were nine milk processors and me. These were hands-on manufacturing guys—all over 40, most over 50, some over 60. Nice men. Smart men. Quiet, competent men. Men with a sense of humor and self-worth. Men who would make unshakable allies and remorseless enemies. Men who drove Suburbans and were still married to their original wives. Men whose careers

THREE SPECIES OF ADVERTISING

At the risk of demystifying the creative process and of alienating most of the ad agency world, I'll state that virtually all advertising falls into one or a combination of three approaches: information, association, or reflection.

Advertising Information is the oldest method of selling. As the name implies, it attempts to sell something (anything from condos to condoms) by providing a tidbit of information (often disguised as fact). Claims are the delivery vehicles for these tidbits. We are all too familiar with these claims. Food A not only has fewer calories, but tastes great. Food B not only tastes great, but has fewer calories. Medicine A relieves headaches ten times faster than Medicine B. Medicine B lasts five times longer than Medicine A. The claims go on ad nauseum.

Unless one has a new and incredibly relevant piece of information, this type of advertising is redundant, regressive, and usually a massive waste of time and money. But it sure makes the guy who made up the claim feel proud.

Advertising by Association is generally more fun, but seldom more effective. Let's see, we make basketball shoes, so why don't we pay the greatest basketball players in the world to wear our

hinged on how well they could process and distribute millions upon millions of gallons of milk—every day of every week of every month. The cows that supplied them didn't take vacation breaks, and they either gave milk or became Happy Meals. (Few people realize that dairy cattle don't retire, they get made into ground beef patties.)

Facing us were the agency people—people not far removed from their stereotype. Predominantly men, with a sprinkling of women. Few had reached 40; several were under 30 (mere adolescents to the processors). They were well dressed and well groomed, some almost stylized. A mix of Armani, Land's End, and Eddie

shoes and pitch our products? Not a bad idea, until the other three shoe companies do exactly the same thing. How about showing our bank's financial services being used by a really successful looking (read rich and handsome) guy driving a car that costs more than the GNP of many developing nations? Or what if we were to put our new line of fall clothing on some truly exquisite women standing, lying, and squatting in suggestive, provocative positions? Gee, no one has ever done that before.

As you can tell, advertising by association isn't my favorite approach, mostly because it gets incredibly repetitive and predictable. Just how many times can we recycle the same idea before the "numbness/dumbness" buzzer goes off?

Advertising by Reflection is a more elusive animal. There wasn't much of this type of advertising before the GOT MILK? campaign. It is founded, not on convincing people of something, but on reminding them of a truth that they have forgotten or simply overlooked. Like what a pain in the butt it is to run out of milk when your bowl is full of corn flakes. Or the fact that your kid can't dunk her Oreos in iced tea. Or that bolting down just-baked chocolate chip cookies without milk verges on inhuman. All GOT MILK? advertising does is reflect, dramatize, and grossly magnify what we already hold true.

Bauer. Most of these men drove high-performance German cars, and more than a few had prior wives from prior lives. They were smooth, slick, and completely alien to my board.

A couple of the agencies worked hard to eliminate themselves. One group attempted, despite all my instructions to the contrary, to spoon-feed us another "good for you" strategy. They proved immovable — what I call "client deaf." No matter how often or strongly I nudged them toward Food & Milk, they relentlessly circled back to the benefits of calcium and nonfat milk.

Another group talked in first-person plural for about 90 minutes without once uttering (pun intended) the word "milk." They spoke of their many advertising successes in cars and jeans and computers. They spoke of their unparalleled research capabilities. Mostly they spoke of themselves. Two down.

The third agency came across as smart, pragmatic, sales driven, and creative. They had studied the milk business, taken my guidance to heart, and come up with some intriguing ways of selling milk. I came close to recommending them. Problem: When asked tough, probing questions, they became adversarial, almost combative. They were a difficult bunch of guys to like.

Goodby Who?

And then there was Goodby, Berlin & Silverstein. For simplicity's sake, I'll call them by their current name,

There were no MBAs. No account guys. No "empty suits."

GS&P (Goodby, Silverstein & Partners). They brought five people, roughly half the number brought by the other agencies. All the principals were with us (Andy Berlin still had his name on the door but had left the agency). One was a Brit by the name of Jon Steel. His title was something inconclusive, like director of account planning. Jon made an immediate and immutable impression on my board. Rather than personalize the milk challenge, he was able to disassociate himself from it, to look at it almost clinically. This objective, detached approach allowed him to ingest and digest how everyday folks felt about milk. Jon didn't use the word "I" once and stayed firmly affixed to the subject of selling milk. He combined confidence with humility, qualities seldom found in tandem. I liked him immediately. Jon was to become our "food no milk" champion.

Rich Silverstein was a sliver of a guy. Turbo-charged, he launched rather than merely spoke his words, and visibly squirmed in his seat. I expected him to leave skid marks on the floor when he stood to present. He called to mind a type-A toddler with a mustache. In hindsight, we should have set up a stationary bike for him, as we discovered that Rich is a highly competitive (some say compulsive) cyclist.

Jeff Goodby and Rich Silverstein

Jeff Goodby was a different species. I could write a short book on him. Instead, let's do it in less than 50 words. Devoted family man. Hurtling toward 50. Shoulder-length hair. Artist. Writer. Reporter. Commercial director. Treasures humor. Doesn't sleep. Never stops thinking. Loves fishing. Seldom fishes. Humble and unpretentious. Intense listener. Fearless. Decent third baseman (I should know, I played first). Came up with the line "GOT MILK?"

Goodby's firm was, by agency standards, in its adolescence. Founded in 1983 by Jeff Goodby, Rich Silverstein, and Andy Berlin, it was a spin-off from Hal Riney & Partners, itself an offshoot of Ogilvy & Mather. (Some of the most creative and respected agencies of the past 20 years have been the offspring of mega-agencies.) The people who ran GS&P were also writers and art directors, people who actually created ads. There were no MBAs. No account guys. No "empty suits." Goodby and his partners submerged themselves in advertising. They wrote.

They drew. They recorded. They edited. They produced and directed. They also learned to use the copy and fax machines. They had, and continue to have, an obsessive, personal investment in their work. Located on the West Coast, GS&P was thousands of miles and a million "thought years" away from the formulaic ad agencies in New York and Chicago.

To quote *Adweek*'s 20th anniversary issue (November 9, 1998): "It [GS&P] started with $8,000 from maxed-out credit cards . . . and a simple notion: Assemble a group of people to create ideas more associated with individuals, art, and social forces than with market research. They proved an agency could achieve creative excellence and also be wildly successful without being on Madison Avenue."

Here are a few select words from the GS&P mission:

We want to be the best advertising agency in the world, as judged by our peers and by our effect on the marketplace. We don't want to be the biggest, but are determined to be consistently better than other agencies, and always better than we just were ourselves. Our pursuit of these aims is governed by one overriding belief: that the work always comes first.

Putting Milk First

For the prospective milk account, the creative people at GS&P came up with the brilliant idea of deprivation, the absence of milk.

The human experience of deprivation stretches all the way back to our primeval roots, to our shivering, hungry ancestors. It starts with conception; nothing is more vulnerable to deprivation than a fetus. Birth itself introduces us to deprivation in two big ways. Once that cord is cut, we need oxygen and we need it fast. That essential supplied, we soon cry out for you know what—milk. Deprive us for long and the decibel level reaches new heights. At this point in life, milk deprivation is not the least bit funny. All levity is lost on an empty stomach.

Normally associated with hunger, cold, and other suffering, deprivation is something to be avoided, akin to a curse. It is a strange, verging on weird way to sell a product, especially one as plentiful as milk. The folks from GS&P employed a clever maneuver to introduce the concept of milk deprivation to my board. Rather than spell it out in bold letters on a slide or chart, rather than try to "prove" it with reams of data and multicolored graphs, rather than appeal to our intellect or try

> Deprivation is something to be avoided, akin to a curse. It is a strange, verging on weird way to sell a product, especially one as plentiful as milk.

to reason us into submission, they simply pushed the PLAY button on the video machine.

The first image that came up on the screen made me feel like I was a head of lettuce or bottle of ketchup. We were looking out into a small room, apparently a kitchen, from the interior of a refrigerator. Yep, from inside the refrigerator. One by one, people—mostly young, urban types—stuck their noses into the fridge and started searching for something. Something that was always there. At first they were smiling and a bit groggy. But as they realized "it" was missing, they became progressively more agitated. Frowns turned to sneers, and some unmentionable words were used. Finally, they clawed their way into the depths of the fridge, pushing aside the usual assortment of bag lunches, soda, and condiments in search of "it." Oh yes, and they were all holding a bowl of cereal. The "it," of course, was milk.

It seems that, in preparation for the milk pitch, Jon Steel had observed how people in his office consumed milk. The results were striking. Men outnumbered women two to one in milk consumption. Most usage was before 10 A.M., on cereal. Almost all consumption was paired with food. Also revealing was the habitual nature of the food and milk behavior. Day after day, the same people downed milk in the same manner at just about the same time.

Then the mischievous Mr. Steel had an idea. He emptied the agency's refrigerator of all its milk, cut a hole in the back wall of the fridge, and installed a video camera. In this way, it was possible to tape people searching for the milk without their knowing it. Dozens of Goodby people, accustomed to kicking off their day with Cap'n Crunch or Cocoa Puffs, were left stranded, without milk. Dozens more, mouths full of cookies or brownies, found that their afternoon snack had been destroyed. Deprived, they became more than a little pissed off. Their reactions, raw and unedited, made up the first milk deprivation video.

My board's response to the candid, graphic display of milk deprivation was truly telling. Rather than react as milk processors or business leaders or prospective clients, they reacted like people. They laughed. The full-bodied, "I know this could have been me" kind of laughter that only accompanies a truism. One processor managed to stop chuckling long enough to tell his own deprivation tale.

The week before, his wife had baked chocolate chip cookies for their prolific clan. The aroma of warm, gooey cookies filled the house, and drooling kids were lining up outside the kitchen. As the matriarch stacked the cookies, she asked her husband to grab some milk from the fridge. Remember, this is a man whose plant fills a gallon of milk every few seconds. He opened the refrigerator, only to find a lonely quart of nonfat and a pint of half-and-half. Rather than face wrath, rage, and embarrassment, he tore out the back door and bought three gallons of milk at the local gas station. He was saved, except that it was his competitor's brand of milk.

Snapple on Your Wheaties?

Building on their successful presentation of milk deprivation, Goodby then asked some silly but incisive questions that to this day make me giggle. Ever try pouring Snapple on your Wheaties? Or dunking your freshly baked Tollhouse cookies in 7-Up? Or washing down a fudge brownie with a nice big slug of prune juice?

These questions crystallize how vital milk can be. More than any other nonalcoholic beverage, people become dependent on milk. Milk for their coffee or cereal or with chocolate. Take their milk away and their lives begin to crumble. Milk deprivation is analogous to air deprivation. Except in places like Los Angeles and Mexico City, air is invisible. We spend our entire lives breathing the stuff and hardly give it a thought. But jump in a pool and hold your breath under-water. At about the one-minute mark, your lungs begin to burn, and the survival mechanism kicks in. Instantly, air rises to the top of your list of priorities. Over the next minute, the vet appointment, the PTA meeting, and even the upcoming business trip drop, not just to the bottom, but right off the list.

Milk deprivation worked as a concept because it was so damn true. And because we personalized the idea. Each of us in that room could recall more than one occasion when we had poured our cereal, sliced our banana, and reached into the refrigerator for milk, only to shake the carton and find it empty, save for a few ounces of "backwash" from our teenager's last swig. As with other asic needs we normally take for granted (air, food, shelter), we realized that the only time we thought hard about milk was when we had run out of it.

Milk deprivation worked as a concept because it was so damn true.

Goodby had brought us milk deprivation. They had walked into that room in Southern California armed with an advertising bullet far more powerful than they, or we, had a right to expect. Did we recognize its power immediately? Did my board and I jump out of our seats, applaud, and hand GS&P the milk account? I have to confess the answer is no.

We actually spent a fair amount of time discussing the agency selection. The race came down to Goodby and the talented but combative agency. We debated the pros and cons, strengths and weaknesses. Finally, after 14 hours of sitting in that sweaty little room, chairman Dick said, "Let Manning make the decision. He's going to have to live with them." Based on a reel of commercials, a room full of genuinely nice people, and a funny idea called milk deprivation, we selected GS&P. And we've never looked back.

got milk?

chapter 3

Creative Gene Pool

was disappointed. After spending the last month carefully choreographing an agency review, I was ready to assign the milk account (and finally become someone's client). And Jeff Goodby was out of town. The operator passed me on to Jeff's creative alter ego, Rich Silverstein. True to form, Rich was incredibly polite and almost apologetic, as if he were preparing himself for bad news. It was endearing. Here was one of the most talented creative people in the business and, rather than expecting to win, he actually thought they had lost the pitch. I informed him otherwise. His reaction was, "You've got to be kidding! No way! We won?" So I told him again, "You're in the milk business." I also casually reminded him that, no pressure intended, we needed the best TV campaign in America in about ten weeks.

Selecting GS&P in 1993 was like handing a little-known but highly gifted sculptor a chunk of top-quality marble, some new tools, and the charge to chisel and cleave the next David. The first step in sculpting GOT MILK? was a simple research technique called focus groups. These groups are the equivalent of an umbilical

cord to consumers, allowing us to continually take the creative pulse of an advertising campaign.

How did the GOT MILK? focus groups work? Simple. Eight or ten people came to a central location (usually in a shopping mall), signed in, and were escorted to a really boring conference room that was equipped with an overhead microphone, a videotape camera, and a floor-to-ceiling mirror. The moderator, Jon Steel, warmed everyone up with small talk about names, family size, occupation, etc.

At this point, Jon's radar screen was working overtime, seeking out obsessive/compulsive talkers, people who would dominate and destroy the focus group. He smoothly shifted gears and began probing how the participants felt about advertising in general, and beverage ads in particular. He then got down to business: exploring milk and milk deprivation. The mirror was one-way,

We needed the best TV campaign in America in about ten weeks.

allowing people behind the glass (such as me) to see in, but not to be seen. I was accompanied by clusters of agency people. I remember two who spent their time giggling like adolescents, making crude remarks, and stuffing their faces with M&Ms. I silenced them with a none-too-subtle query about what "other account" they might like to work on.

The first round of eight GOT MILK? focus groups was conducted in July 1993. Held throughout California, the groups included adults, teens, and kids. We got lucky. People made it clear that they didn't need reminding that milk was good for them, that it was high in calcium and kids needed it to grow up big and strong. They also revealed that they regarded milk as infantile, innocent, and incredibly boring. Pure to the point of virginal, it lacked an

edge or attitude. It certainly wasn't cool. Teens mumbled about being embarrassed to drink it in public.

Deprivation Blues

Our intuition was confirmed when, in group after group, people stated unequivocally that cereal, cookies, peanut butter, and anything chocolate drove them to milk. And they strongly reinforced the notion that the only time people thought about milk was when they ran out, when they were deprived of it. A young man in his mid-20s said it best: "If you've got freshly baked cookies, you've got to have milk. No milk, no cookies." A teen fired back across the table: "You've got this bowl of Cheerios. It's nothing. But add milk

got milk?

OUT OF WHITE

One woman told of being trapped by a huge snowstorm in her California mountain community: whiteout conditions, lots of howling wind. Her husband and two kids were already at home, tending a roaring fire and a cauldron of split pea and sausage soup. Mom's job was to swing by the grocery store and stock up on the essentials—milk, bread, diapers, and a case of drinkable Merlot—before the storm closed the roads.

Undaunted by the blizzard, the woman spent a few minutes working out the four-wheel drive mechanism on her SUV, finally got the differential locked, and set off. She found her way to the local grocery, remembered to park so as to allow escape, exchanged the necessary niceties with the clerk, and shopped. No need for a list. She was only after the essentials.

Home she went, plowing through snowdrifts, avoiding fallen trees, helping stranded drivers with calls to the local police.

Finally, she saw her cozy little home glowing through the swirls of white. She honked a greeting, then trekked up the path to the house. It was treacherous; her purse and grocery bags nearly slipped from her grip, but she made the porch stairs without calamity. The storm had heightened and she was truly grateful to be home. Her mind skipped ahead a few hours. Kids asleep, the down comforter spread before the glowing embers, she and her hubby sipping Merlot. The door swung open to reveal her radiant family. Damn, she was glad not to have to go out again for two, maybe three days.

Dad spread his arms and said, "Thanks for shopping, Sweetie. I don't think we could have made it without milk." After a torturous silence, she put down the groceries, backed into the storm, started the car, and headed back to the supermarket.

and it's everything." This same young man testified to occasionally consuming an entire box of cereal and a half-gallon of milk for an afternoon snack. (If only we could have cloned that kid.)

We also used the groups as sounding boards for the "GOT MILK?" phrase. Like a dream come true, virtually all respondents said that it reminded them instantly of just how distressing and disabling running out of milk could be. They then volunteered that, upon seeing or hearing "GOT MILK?," they would check the fridge, shake the carton, and buy more milk. They also related stories, often intimate and hilarious, of their own milk deprivation.

The purpose of these initial focus groups was not to test advertising ideas—we didn't yet have advertising

Copy strategies, as perfected by the monolithic consumer product companies, are cerebral, lifeless, rigid, humorless, and sterile strings of words.

ideas. Rather, it was to cast milk deprivation in consumer language and to help us construct something called the GOT MILK? Creative Brief. Drafted and crafted by the advertising agency, it was a compilation of core questions and answers that would serve as the launchpad for the GOT MILK? campaign.

A Creative Brief in Brief

While a brilliant brief is not a guarantee of a brilliant campaign, it's far better than a traditional copy strategy. Copy strategies, as perfected by the monolithic consumer product companies, are cerebral, lifeless, rigid, humorless, and sterile strings of words. While serving as a workable exposition of what the client wants the advertising to say, a really "tight" copy strategy has castrated many a creative thought (and has sent many a writer and art director running for cover).

The Old Way: The Copy Strategy

To dramatize the importance of the creative brief to GOT MILK?, let's write the milk deprivation copy strategy the old way, more in line with traditional packaged goods.

- The purpose of the advertising is to convince target users to buy and consume more milk.

- The reason is that running out of milk is extremely disruptive to family life.

- The primary target for the advertising is women, 18 to 49, with kids under 18.

- The work will be humorous and witty, but always in good taste.

- The milk carton must be shown in every commercial, preferably twice, close up.

- The word "milk" must be said at least three times.

- The "GOT MILK?" tag line must be on the screen for at least 2.75 seconds.

The New Way: The GS&P Creative Brief

Now let's look at the original GOT MILK? Creative Brief, written after our first series of focus groups in June 1993.

Q Why advertise at all?

Milk sales are going down. We need them to go up.

Q What is the advertising supposed to do?

Get people to consume more milk when they're at home and buy more milk (or buy it more often) when they're at the store. Over 90 percent of all milk is consumed at home. This is where we stand a chance of defending and possibly expanding our business.

Q What is the advertising not supposed to do?

Change beliefs and attitudes. Advertising probably can't improve much on nutritional beliefs; over 90 percent of people already believe milk is good for them. Any nutritional message we attempt to send them will be taken as redundant to what they already know. Through advertising, we probably can't convince fat-phobic girls and women that the 90 calories in a glass of nonfat milk is as good a diet choice as Diet Coke or bottled water. We probably can't even convince parents that milk is the only beverage they should allow their kids to drink.

We also probably can't change attitudes about milk consumed outside the home. In a world of mega-brands like Coke and Pepsi and Snapple, it's unlikely we can convince teenagers that milk is a cool choice when hanging out at Burger King or McDonald's. Nor can we expect to convince adults to order milk instead of coffee or iced tea at their favorite restaurants or drink milk in place of beer at the ball park.

got milk?

Who are we talking to?

Anyone who already consumes milk and doesn't hate it. Women are more important than men since they buy the vast majority of the milk. But since men, teens, and kids drink tons of it, we need to talk to them too.

What do we know about consumers that will help us?

People don't think about milk until they need it and don't have it. These are times when only milk will do, when there is simply no substitute. These are times centered around specific foods and eating occasions. Cereal for breakfast. Cookies, brownies, and pastries for snacks and desserts. Peanut butter and jelly sandwiches for lunch. Coffee and espresso drinks (remember, we were in California). Any form of chocolate, any time.

On all of these occasions, being caught without milk is a frustrating, even torturous experience. Running out of milk in the morning can ruin the entire day before it begins. A mouthful of peanut butter can be sheer anguish without

got milk?

TOM MAYER

milk to cut through it. We have learned that if people have lots of milk in the fridge, they will find a way to use it up. Conversely, if they are running low, they will pace their consumption, giving priority to their kids' needs.

Q What is the main thing we need to communicate?

There are times when only milk will do, when milk is irreplaceable. Running out will lead to angst, anger, and general chaos. So, buy more milk and, while you're at it, break out the Oreos right now.

Q How will we measure the advertising?

People will remember it. They'll like it. They'll think it's funny and true. They'll buy a little more milk the next time they shop. They'll check the fridge to see if they have enough. They'll choose cookies and milk instead of chips and a Coke. Milk sales will stop hemorrhaging and eventually go up.

Comparing the GS&P creative brief and the old copy strategy, which approach would you prefer to follow? Which set of words would ignite your creativity? Which would energize and inspire you? Which would liberate the ideas simmering in the recesses of your mind? Not surprisingly, my vote goes to the creative brief.

Meeting of the Minds

Having worked so hard to develop the brief, the creative teams at Goodby promptly ignored it and began cranking out a crazed assortment of GOT MILK? ideas.

GOT MILK? was an idea on the altar. Naked, stripped of pretense and protection, it was going to either live or die in the marketplace. But beyond being a good way to sell milk, GOT MILK? was a testament to the power of ideation. For from child development to software development,

Creative people, like those who spawned got milk?, will devour tradition and recast life as we know it.

ideas will define success in the next decade. Ideas will displace models, dispel "truths," and demolish boundaries. Creative people, like those who spawned GOT MILK?, will devour tradition and recast life as we know it.

Unfortunately, there is a gaping void. Few people are talking about how to manage all those creative minds—minds that seldom operate in a linear, logical fashion but float, digress, climax, retreat, and surge according to their own mysterious undercurrents, and minds that are, as one quickly discovers, often connected to incredibly fragile egos and esteems.

GOT MILK?, or more accurately, the GOT MILK? creative process was a small step toward filling that void. Since the conception and birth of GOT MILK? commercials were so purely and, at times, painfully creative, they provided us with a unique chance to manage and mismanage creative minds. And since advertising is by far the most intensely human part of big business, the lessons learned can be as easily applied to raising kids as to raising capital.

To understand the GOT MILK? creative process, one needs to seek the origins of creativity. I believe that whoever said necessity is the mother of invention was grossly understating the obvious. Survival, as in "Will my family and I live through the night?" was the progenitor of creativity. It must have become frighteningly clear to some cave person that sheer brawn was not going to carry the day against volcanic eruptions, hostile neighbors, and toothy carnivores. Humans needed an inside advantage, and creativity was their genetic trump card. Tools and fire, weapons and a

wardrobe were all great ideas that, I would propose, were born of the urge for survival. So was GOT MILK? Milk processors were endangered, their survival threatened. Something was needed to fend off the ravenous competition. GOT MILK? was that something.

• • •

The people behind GOT MILK? were compulsive idea machines. They had no choice and no control. GOT MILK? ideas bubbled up from some cauldron within them. And once these ideas started ricocheting off the walls of their minds, they were compelled to write them or sing them or draw them or, at the very least, scream them at someone. It was an addiction. If you stepped into their line of fire, you got their ideas. This compulsion is what sets them apart from people who merely have good ideas from time to time.

Since advertising is **by far the most** intensely **human part of** big business, **the lessons** learned can be **as easily applied** to raising kids **as to raising** capital.

As if adhering to some unspoken law, most advertising is created by teams. Usually an art director and copywriter, these teams virtually live together (much to the dismay of spouses and significant others) when working on a large assignment. By having two, three, or even four creative teams working on the same project, the creative director (Jeff Goodby, in our case) not only gets a multitude of ideas and perspectives, but also creates a friendly competition within the agency. Like all competitive beasts, creative people often work harder and longer (albeit not always more intelligently) when in a race. This race was for milk.

The Goodby teams were young, urban, hip people with hyperactive imaginations and no kids. And, for the prospective milk account, all guys—Chuck and Harry, Erich and Joe. This was a prime creative assignment and, while not officially a competition, the masculine, competitive juices were running high. Although no one knew it at the time, that first pool of GOT MILK? commercials would

not only help lift Goodby, Silverstein & Partners to national prominence, it would launch several careers.

But before this crew could get their ideas in front of Jeff Manning, they had to get them past Jeff Goodby. Getting Goodby to buy a GOT MILK? idea wasn't actually *that* tough. The idea only needed to be completely unexpected, impossibly intelligent, and universally funny. And it had to be founded in milk deprivation. The really tough job was getting me to bless it. The

Goodby teams would get their chance about two weeks after the creative brief was completed.

I remember the occasion well. We met at the GS&P offices, in one of the older, more interesting brick buildings in San Francisco. I was outnumbered nine or ten to one. The account planner presented the creative brief, silently praying that I wouldn't conveniently forget I had approved it or, worse yet, change the objective. Yes, the strategy was milk deprivation. Yes, the target was people who currently liked and consumed milk. Yes, the tag line was "GOT MILK?" Yes, yes, yes. I was desperate to get beyond the strategic foreplay and into advertising ideas. Jeff Goodby must have picked up on my body language because he broke into the discussion, said they had six spots to present, and nodded to Chuck, a writer with flaming red hair.

The creative teams had paraded in wearing baggy jeans, T-shirts, and worn-out running shoes. (This was in midsummer 1993, before the law was passed that really cool, young San Francisco ad people had to dress in all black.) They carried nothing but a few scraps of paper. No videotapes, no wall-sized presentation boards, no music scores, no exciting visual concepts. The scraps turned out to be scripts for 30-second commercials. Some were typed, some scribbled; a few included primitive drawings, indications of a location or set. At least this agency wasn't afraid to let their advertising ideas stand on their own.

Chuck smiled, said something about how neat it was to work on the milk business, and started describing an esoteric bit of American history. The commercial was about a weird, isolated young man who had dedicated his life, as well as his apartment, to the life,

times, and death of Alexander Hamilton. (As I was to discover over the next year, death was one of Chuck's favorite themes.)

The Birth of "Aaron Burr"

As the story unfolded, it became clear that I was not at all prepared for the kind of GOT MILK? advertising Goodby was going to give us. My mind went into fast forward. What did Alexander Hamilton and his dueling partner Aaron Burr have to do with selling milk? We were mass marketing to 33 million Californians. Even in this

notes from the set

Commercial #1: Aaron Burr

Had a heated argument about the size and nature of the peanut butter knife. The prop people had stuck a carving knife of some 12 inches into an industrial-sized jar of peanut butter. I thought it was too frightening to see this strange character spreading a sandwich with a tool that could have butchered a hog, but I gave in. Looking back, I laugh at my hesitation. The blade was perfect and not the least bit terrifying.

We also had a debate about how much peanut butter we should stuff into our protagonist's mouth and whether or not we should see the gooey, sticky brown mess as he spoke. We tried it several ways and, good taste aside, opted to let him talk with his mouth full and open. It was a crucial decision, as it perfectly set up his desperate cry for milk and pitiful utterance of "Aaaawon Buuuhh."

BABY & CAT

VIDEO

OPEN ON CAT CLOCK TICKING. CUT TO MAN WALKING INTO KITCHEN IN BATHROBE, POV FROM BEHIND BABY SITTING IN BABY CHAIR AT SET BREAKFAST TABLE. IT'S MORNING TIME. HE WAVES TO THE BABY.

CUT TO BABY SUCKING DOWN MILK FROM BOTTLE, POV FROM MAN.

CUT TO REAR VIEW OF CAT ON KITCHEN COUNTER WALKING TOWARD MILK BOWL.

CUT TO POV OF CEREAL BOWL AS MAN POURS CEREAL.

CUT BACK TO BABY SUCKING MILK BOTTLE.

CUT TO MAN WATCHING BABY WHILE LIFTING MILK CARTON OVER CEREAL. ONLY A TINY SPLASH OF MILK COMES OUT OF EMPTY CARTON. PAN IN TO CU OF MILK DROP ON LIP OF MILK CARTON BEING HELD DIRECTLY IN FRONT OF MAN'S RIGHT EYE.

CUT BACK TO MAN'S POV OF BABY SUCKING MILK BOTTLE. IN FOREFRONT IS MAN'S BOWL OF DRY CEREAL.

QUICK CUT TO OVERHEAD VIEW OF KITCHEN SCENE.

CUT TO CU OF MAN'S FACE STARING INTENTLY AT CAT.

CUT TO CAT LAPPING MILK.

Audio

MAN: "Hey, Boopy!"

SFX: Baby sucking milk.

CAT: "Prrrrrrrr."

SFX: Cereal falling.

SFX: Drop. Fizz.

SFX: Drop.

(Music: Whistled tune from *The Good, the Bad, and the Ugly*)

SFX: Baby sucking milk.

SFX: Cat lapping milk.

VIDEO	**Audio**
QUICK CUT BACK TO CU OF MAN'S FACE. EYES MOVE OVER TO BABY.	SFX: Baby sucking milk.
CUT BACK TO BABY CONTINUING TO SUCK DOWN MILK BOTTLE.	
CUT BACK TO CU OF MAN, HIS HEAD BURIED IN HIS HANDS. HE RUBS HIS FACE WHILE LOOKING UP AT CAT.	SFX: Cat lapping milk.
QUICK CUT BACK TO MAN RUBBING FACE AS HE LOOKS BACK OVER AT BABY.	
CUT BACK TO CAT LAPPING MILK.	
CUT BACK TO BABY SUCKING MILK.	
CUT BACK TO MAN WHO LOOKS BACK AT CAT.	SFX: Cat lapping milk.
CUT TO CAT LAPPING MILK.	SFX: Baby sucking milk.
CUT TO MAN LOOKING BACK AT BABY.	
CUT TO CU OF BABY SUCKING.	
CUT TO POV OF BABY FROM BEHIND BOTTLE AS MAN SLOWLY REACHES FORWARD TOWARD BABY'S BOTTLE.	BABY: "I don't think so, Baldy!"
CUT TO POV OF MAN AS BABY PUTS BOTTLE DOWN. SLOWLY PAN IN ON BABY.	
CUT BACK TO MAN'S STARTLED FACE AS CAMERA SLOWLY PANS IN.	SFX: Startled cat fight hiss.
CUT TO CARD. SUPER IN WHITE ON BLACK: "GOT MILK?"	

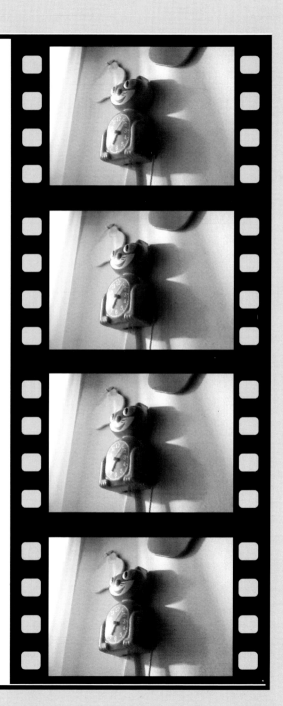

Commercial #2: Couple

Our most subtle spot. Still considered some of the best copywriting in the campaign. But, the production complete, we didn't have an ending and were on the verge of losing the commercial. As originally edited, it simply fizzled out. The man and woman just looked blankly at each other and the "GOT MILK?" popped on the screen.

We needed an ending, some concluding moment that would generate a smile and reinforce how deeply the guy had dug himself in. Jeff Goodby, plowing through hundreds of outtakes, saved the spot, as well as the creative team's rear ends. He uncovered about a second and a half of film where the husband, with no place to hide and nothing to say, simply shrugs and smiles this "I really blew it this time, didn't I?" smile.

Commercial #3: Lifeboat

I am certain that the director (yes, Michael Bay) shot the commercial on an island so he wouldn't have to deal with me or with the creative team. When I had a comment or idea, I would tell Goodby, who in turn would radio the assistant director, who would, I am quite sure, only pretend to tell the director. Those of us left on the mainland spent our time playing tag football. Life must be fair, however, because the lifeboat kept sinking with the full cast aboard. The water was shallow, but we nearly lost an actress in the mud and slime. Eventually the crew patched the boat with cloth tape, but only after the entire cast was thoroughly sodden.

---

well-educated state, no more than a few thousand could have degrees in American history. Were the rest of the agency's ideas this remote, this far removed from the kitchen? I forced myself back into the room and to the story being unfolded for me.

By now the art director, Erich, had begun to paint a word picture (apparently real ad guys don't need real pictures), describing an enormous peanut butter and no jelly sandwich, the painting of Alexander Hamilton on the wall, the panic and desperation of the protagonist as he reaches for his salvation from the eight or ten ounces of peanut butter clinging to the roof of his mouth. But the milk carton is empty, save for a few useless, mocking drops. The once-in-a-lifetime contest opportunity passes him by as he slurs one last "Aaaawon Buuuuhh" into the phone. Erich's vivid painting ended with the ominous dial tone, the scene going black and the words "GOT MILK?" popping out of the blackness in gleaming white letters.

I was unconvinced. Was this going to be the greatest campaign in milk history? I breathed deeply, reached for another chocolate chip cookie, mumbled a request for some milk, and suggested they continue.

"Is This About My Time in Prison?"

Harry and Joe were up next. Looking like an oversized teddy bear in a crisp white T-shirt, Harry, clearly the team leader, was immediately likable. He described what, at the outset, sounded like the most boring commercial on record. He called it "Couple," and described an innocent-looking, wimpy sort of guy in the kitchen. It's the middle of the night and he's peeling a banana as his wife skewers him with her eyes and demands, "Did you think I wouldn't find out?" Squirming, he inadvertently reveals his secrets and lies: "Doesn't a zirconia look just like a real diamond?"; then, "Is this about my time in prison?" No, it's about the fact that he drank the last of the milk. The spot ends with "GOT MILK?"

Sensing my unease, Harry presented the spot again, this time attempting to act out the parts. It was funnier and more convincing when this big guy attempted a woman's voice and limp wrist. It certainly brought some life to the "my time in prison" line. Slowly, ever so slowly, I was beginning to sense the pulse and potential of GOT MILK?

The next script set me back, however. It would have been perfect for the 1997 release of *Titanic*. It was about a lifeboat filled with stranded passengers, graham crackers, and an empty thermos of milk. It didn't make sense,

Commercial #4: Baby & Cat

Brilliant, simple story. Great casting for the dad. Trouble, big trouble, disaster-level trouble: neither of the twin babies would suck on their milk bottles. The mom had just fed them. The problem was compounded by a law that says babies can be on the set for only a few precious hours each day. We were lucky. We dunked the bottles in honey, shot a million feet of film, and got about six seconds of glory.

A few weeks after "Baby & Cat" went on the air, I got a call about the ad from an irate man. After ten minutes of unintelligible screaming and slander, he finally took a breather and I was able to ask what exactly he found so objectionable. It turned out he was incensed at our denigration of bald men. Bald men? I laughed, said that it certainly wasn't our aim to insult anyone and mentioned my own rapidly ebbing hairline.

got milk?

gotmilk.com

wasn't all that funny, and should have died on the spot. But I was trying hard to be open and supportive. (We eventually produced "Lifeboat." It turned out not to make sense and wasn't all that funny. Duhhhh.)

We were all visibly loosening up. I was listening better and smiling more. The Goodby teams were gaining confidence. They must have sensed that this wasn't going to be a creative bloodbath, that maybe this Manning guy might actually "get it" and approve some good work. Back to Erich and Chuck.

The Good, the Bad, and got milk?

Quick on his feet, Chuck pointed out that the next idea was set in a kitchen and no one had to die. "Baby & Cat" was as perfect an expression of milk deprivation as I had heard (or would ever hear). A father, a baby, a cat, a breakfast table, milk for the baby's bottle and the cat's bowl. None for the dad's cereal. Tension builds as Dad considers who is the easier target, his kid or his cat. Music from *The Good, the Bad, and the Ugly* softly builds as he reaches for his child's bottle, only to be frozen in mid-grab by the infant's defiant stare and the line, "I don't think so, Baldy." We end on GOT MILK? and a cat's screech. No one needed to explain this script to me, and the creative folks knew they had sold one.

Overbite

In our fixation on television, we had forgotten about outdoor creative (ad lingo for billboards, bus shelters, and signs on trains and buses). An art director with a mischievous, elfin smile spoke up. They had an idea, a somewhat unusual idea. He reached for a set of presentation boards I hadn't noticed. As he unveiled them, I first smiled, then laughed outright. No explanation was given, none was necessary. Lined up along the

How would regular folks in smaller, more rural communities like Ukiah, Modesto, and Redding respond to got milk?

conference room wall were a gingerbread man, a graham cracker, a baking tin of brownies, and the most scrumptious chocolate chip cookie imaginable. What made me laugh was the fact that each piece of food was missing a big bite, and in its place were those two little words and a question mark. Nothing could have expressed milk deprivation better.

At that moment, it was clear to me that the idea of milk deprivation wasn't created, invented, or manufactured. Rather, it was discovered or, more accurately, unearthed. Now that it was above ground, we had to clean up the concept. Chip off the goo and garbage disguising it. Scrub it, rinse it, and polish it. Reveal its many facets. Milk deprivation really was a gem of a truth, lying just below the surface of our everyday experience.

The meeting was winding down. We talked about changes to the scripts, commercial directors we might use, and how soon we needed to get this campaign on every TV screen in California. We were all excited, although I still harbored serious reservations about "Aaron Burr," "Lifeboat," and "Couple." The ideas were funny and certainly founded on the deprivation theme, but were we talking to our urban selves? How would regular folks in the suburbs of Los Angeles and San Francisco and in smaller, more rural communities like Ukiah, Modesto, and Redding respond? Would they giggle? Would they talk about GOT MILK? Would they check their refrigerators for milk? Would they shake those cartons? Would they reach for the Oreos instead of the pretzels? And would they buy more milk? I had

absolutely no idea. But we were sure going to find out before I stood up in front of my board and recommended some $3 million in television production.

As a disaster check, and to gain insight into how normal folks felt about the work, we bounced these ideas, nothing but typed scripts, off 40 or 50 people around California. As I would do more than a hundred times over the next six years, I sat behind the one-way mirror. Keeping my expectations low (a defensive tactic of mine),

I half-expected people to find the spots irrelevant, confusing, or even in bad taste. I mean the guy in "Aaron Burr" talked with his mouth full, the father in "Baby & Cat" tried to steal his child's milk, and the anti-hero in "Couple" was an ex-convict who deceived his wife.

My reservations proved groundless. People, from teens to grandparents, shook with laughter. They understood milk deprivation. They loved the wacky, unexpected situations. They appreciated the wit and intelligence. They drooled over the food, even if they were only photographs. They felt the horror of running out of milk. They even felt the moment of angst of picking up and shaking an empty carton. But best of all, they told us that these GOT MILK? commercials, even in their most primitive scripted forms, would get them to buy and consume more milk. The GOT MILK? campaign was born. Now, it needed to be produced.

Definitely Not a "Bored Meeting"

But first, my board had to review and approve the pool of commercials. Remember, these nine gentlemen all worked 50 to 60 hours a week helping to process the 740 million gallons of drinking milk that Californians gulp down each year. They were manufacturing and operations guys, not

Commercial #5: Kid Vendor

This was the first spot in which we used kids, lots of them. The story was about an enterprising little girl who sets up a milk stand adjacent to a homemade-cookie sale. All the kids in the neighborhood have bought cookies for 25¢ apiece. Now dozens of them line up to buy their milk at a significant markup. We had three problems: one, the spot really wasn't about milk deprivation; two, getting the kids to perform was commercial torture; and three, while charming in its own way, it wasn't funny. We ended up producing a version shot with a Super 8-millimeter camera and black and white film. The spot ran for a month and was retired to the commercial graveyard. (It would be interesting to resurrect and run this spot today. Given how pervasive GOT MILK? has become, it just might work now.)

---

advertising VPs. My advice to Jeff Goodby ("advice" might be a bit of an understatement) was to limit the presenters to Jon Steel and himself, both of whom the board had met during the agency review. Jeff astutely asked, "Should we draw storyboards to help them follow the flow of each spot?" While the suggestion was tempting, it struck me that if the ideas were strong enough, clear enough, and funny enough, the board members would get them unaided. Following the focus groups, we had refined the scripts, deleted some unnecessary verbiage, and made the visual descriptions clearer. We would present scripts to the board.

The meeting, held in August in yet another bland and forgettable hotel room, went amazingly well, as well as any creative meeting could possibly go. My faith in Goodby and Steel was validated. They presented the ideas with grace, humility, confidence, and humor. My faith in the advertising ideas was also validated. They were smart and funny. Finally, my faith in the board was completely validated. They listened, understood, and laughed. They

VIDEO

OPEN ON YOUNG MAN SITTING DOWN AT COUNTER OF BOISTEROUS, AMERICAN DINER. HE'S EATING LARGE STACK OF PANCAKES.

CUT TO POV OF YOUNG MAN AS COOK SLAMS GLASS OF ICE WATER DOWN ON COUNTER DIRECTLY IN FRONT OF HIM.

CUT TO CU OF YOUNG MAN WITH MOUTH FULL OF PANCAKE LOOKING UP AT COOK.

CUT TO SIDE VIEW (POV FROM END OF COUNTER) OF WAITER TALKING TO YOUNG MAN WHILE POINTING AT WOMAN NEXT TO YOUNG MAN, SITTING AT COUNTER WITH FOOD AND GLASS OF MILK IN FRONT OF HER.

CUT TO CU OF YOUNG MAN LOOKING OVER AT WOMAN AS SHE GETS UP AND LEAVES THE COUNTER.

CUT TO FULL SHOT OF YOUNG MAN PLACING FORK DOWN IN FRUSTRATION STILL WITH MOUTH FULL, STARING AT HIS ICE WATER.

CUT TO SIDE VIEW OF YOUNG MAN STARING DOWN AT WOMAN'S FULL GLASS OF MILK.

CUT TO CU OF YOUNG MAN STARING AT GLASS, STILL CHEWING PANCAKES. HE LOOKS OVER TO RIGHT TO CHECK IF WOMAN IS STILL GONE.

CUT TO CU OF MILK GLASS AS YOUNG MAN'S HAND GRABS GLASS AND SLIDES IT DOWN COUNTER TOWARDS HIM.

CUT TO FRONT SHOT OF YOUNG MAN PICKING UP GLASS AND DRINKING MILK.

Audio

(MUSIC UNDER THROUGHOUT: "GROOVE ME")

YOUNG MAN (WITH MOUTH FULL): "Could I get some milk, please?"

COOK: "She got the last one."

WOMAN (TO COOK): "Excuse me. I'll be right back, O.K.?"

COOK VO: "I need two specials!"

VIDEO	**Audio**
CUT TO SIDE VIEW OF YOUNG MAN DRINKING MILK AND THEN PUTTING IT DOWN.	
CUT TO SHOT OF YOUNG MAN STARING DOWN AT 1/2 EMPTY GLASS OF MILK AS SEEN THROUGH THE GLASS (POV DIRECTLY BEHIND GLASS). HE LEANS FORWARD TOWARD MILK GLASS AND MOANS AS IF JUST REALIZING WHAT HE HAS DONE.	
CUT TO FRONT VIEW OF YOUNG MAN PICKING UP GLASS OF ICE WATER, AND WHILE HOLDING ICE BACK WITH KNIFE REFILLING MILK GLASS WITH WATER.	YOUNG MAN: "Mmmmmohhhh!"
CUT TO ABOVE VIEW OF YOUNG MAN POURING WATER AS A BIG MAN SITS DOWN WHERE WOMAN WAS SITTING, STARING AT CUSTOMER POURING ICEWATER.	
CUT TO CU OF GLASS WITH KNIFE HOLDING ICE AS WATER POURS.	
CUT TO ABOVE SHOT AS YOUNG MAN SLIDES GLASS OF MILK BACK TOWARD WOMAN'S PLATE IN FRONT OF BIG MAN WITHOUT NOTICING HIM.	
CUT TO NEW CU OF BIG MAN, STILL MYSTIFIED, CONTINUING TO STARE AT YOUNG MAN.	
JUST THEN THE WOMAN RETURNS. SHE KISSES AND HUGS THE BIG MAN. THE BIG MAN JUST KEEPS GLARING AT YOUNG MAN.	WOMAN: "Hi, sweet."
CUT TO ABOVE SHOT AS YOUNG MAN REALIZES THE BIG MAN CAUGHT HIM. HE LOOKS UP AND AWAY IN FEAR.	SFX: plates breaking
FADE TO BLACK. SUPER: "GOT MILK?"	YOUNG MAN (VO): "Check Please."

THE MILLION-DOLLAR MINUTE: HOW MEDIA IS BOUGHT AND SOLD AND WHY YOU SHOULD CARE

A million dollars per minute is now an understatement. Sixty seconds of advertising time during the broadcast of the 1998 Super Bowl sold for around $1.6 million—and soft drink and beer advertisers fought to spend it.

The media business is really nothing more than an ancient barter system gone high tech. Networks and stations own TV and radio time. Magazines and newspapers own space. Outdoor companies own billboards, bus shelters, and a slew of miscellaneous other space. Providers of goods and services need the time and space in order to reach masses of people who they hope will buy their stuff.

Advertising agencies operate in "no man's land." They own neither goods nor services, nor do they own the time and space. They are paid, often large sums, to do a job that the media can't and the client won't.

Like much of commerce, the media business was born of greed. Thousands of years ago, some not-so-stupid salesman figured out that the more folks who saw your wares, the better the chance of selling your excess meat or hides or battle-axes.

So, instead of dragging his goods through mountain passes, parched deserts, or beast-infested forests, he set up shop. He picked some pleasant meadow or oasis, optimally at a heavily traveled crossroad. He talked a few of his peers into joining him and, lo and behold, the first shopping mall was born.

The concept reached its zenith in the bazaars of the Middle East. Jerusalem stands as a living monument to this "let the masses come to you" approach to selling.

This ancient trading was driven by many of the same principles that drive the modern media business (and stock market). These include:

Supply and demand

Staples that were easily grown, manufactured, or stolen had low values and low prices. Items that were at once scarce and prized commanded far higher tolls. Said another way, not many folks were murdered for a bag of spuds, rice, or flour. Thousands died (and countries changed hands) for precious metals and spices. If there were ten Super Bowls per year, the cost per minute would be much lower.

Everything has a price and every price is negotiable

While lots of factors go into price, the golden rule of economics holds. If there are more buyers than supply, price goes up. More supply than buyers, price goes down. In the media world, however, magazines and newspapers tend not to observe the law of supply and demand and "deal" as much as radio and television networks and stations.

Quantity discounts

Buy more (wool, weapons, whips) and you'll get it at a lower price per item. Makes sense. It was more efficient for a seller to unload his inventory to a few large buyers than a gaggle of small ones. He could lower his price to these mass buyers and make money. It's not difficult to imagine the ad: "Special! This Sabbath only. Tender, free-range lambs. Buy two, get the third at half price." Quantity discounts are a huge factor in the media biz today.

Timing is everything

When a buyer made an offer was critical in the markets of old. The cheese seller was far more likely to deal once his goat cheese had begun to ripen and smell. The same went for the produce and meat vendors. Today, it's not a lot different. Media time and space are perishable. The closer a media product gets to "overripe," that is, the air date, the more flexible the seller gets. A network or station is considerably more flexible in their pricing the week before a special is to run than they are six months in advance.

Master these principles and you too could become a media mogul.

also asked probing, intelligent questions intended to improve the work, not tear it down. Six television spots and five outdoor boards were approved. The production process was launched that same day.

We had made a terrific decision in hiring Goodby, Silverstein & Partners. We were about to make another, although I had no clue at the time. The agency sent out the six scripts to an interesting mix of directors (the people who, along with a production company, actually plan and film the commercial). We were limited by time. Our objective was to go on the air within ten weeks, and we were headed into the fourth quarter with its string of holidays and vacations. Many of the top directors were booked solid. We looked at dozens of director reels, compilations of their most recent work.

Goodby strongly favored a lesser-known but talented director named Michael Bay. His reel was full of unusual camera angles and sets, stark, real-people casting, and dark, intelligent humor. He clearly made his mark on the commercials he shot. The destinies of Michael Bay and the GOT MILK? spots were aligned, and he was awarded the job.

I spent a lot of time around Michael over the next two months. Once he got the job, he basically ignored me, giving my ideas and questions lip service at best. I was the client, seemingly one of those pain-in-the-ass guys who get in the way of great work (despite the fact that they pay for it). But I didn't feel singled out; Michael seemed to treat just about everyone on the set that way. That aside, he made a magnificent contribution to that first pool of GOT MILK? spots, especially "Aaron Burr." The lighting, casting, props, and camera work reflected his vision for the commercial.

Media Blitz

While the television and outdoor creative was being produced, the agency's media department was busily placing $20 million in advertising. This is far easier than one would imagine. Not to oversimplify (or diminish) the part played by our media people in the GOT MILK? launch, it really came down to three fundamental questions.

1. Who did we want to reach?

The answer was everyone who didn't hate milk and consumed it at least a few times a week. We weren't going to try to convince people who didn't like and drink milk to change their minds and habits. It would have been futile and even more expensive.

2. Where did we want to reach them?

At home, since 90 percent of all milk is consumed there. To attempt to get people to order milk with their fettucini primavera or Chinese chicken salad at restaurants would have been silly and wasteful. If people didn't drink milk outside the home (with the exception of milk at school), it was because they didn't want to or they preferred other beverages. Truthfully, a Coke does taste better with a burger and fries than a glass of nonfat does. (Restaurants also make ten times as much money

on a glass of soda or iced tea than they do on a glass of milk. Naturally, they aren't disposed to promote milk.)

3. When do we want to reach them?

When they are sitting in front of the TV within 30 feet of the fridge. This is the only time that, assuming GOT MILK? advertising worked, they could actually get up, check their milk supply, and pour some down their throats. It is also when people eat stuff like cookies, cake, and cereal, the foods that drive milk con-

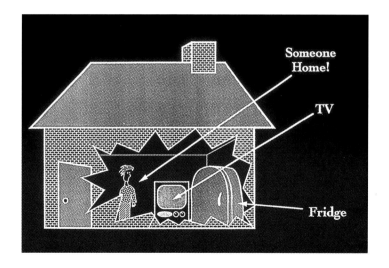

sumption. (The other times we reached people were with outdoor ads on their way home and in the grocery store, when they could choose to buy more milk.)

Armed with three simple questions and their respective answers, the media folks bought millions of dollars of TV advertising at breakfast, afternoon snack, dinner, and evening snack times. (Lunch is eaten outside the home most of the time.) The demographic target (age, gender, family size) for the GOT MILK? advertising changed throughout the day based, you guessed it, on the type of people most likely to be watching TV.

The "Aaron Burr" and "Couple" commercials debuted in October, with one called "Kid Vendor," "Baby & Cat," and "Lifeboat" following in November. To coincide with the television spots, the billboards and bus shelters—featuring the world's most delectable cookie, brownies, and peanut butter and jelly

sandwich—began to appear along highways and streets throughout California.

So, by October 1993, GOT MILK? had an office (in Berkeley, California), an advertising agency, a deprivation strategy, a fabulous pool of commercials, and a media plan. All we didn't have were results. But we didn't have long to wait.

"Honey Nut Cheerios® General Mills

got milk?

chapter 4

A Campaign on Fire

If advertising can catch fire, then got milk? was ablaze by mid-1994. But first, I had to undergo the proverbial trial by fire. The TV spots and billboards had been running for five or six months, and people had begun to take notice, talking about "Aaron Burr," "Baby & Cat," and "Couple" in almost reverential terms. Having been bred in the agency business, I was convinced that, in concert with advertising, public relations was essential to increasing milk sales in California. It was time to launch an aggressive publicity program. It was also time for my "in the box" thinking to trip me up.

The difference between advertising and publicity is often fuzzy. One pays for advertising time and space, a 30-second GOT MILK? commercial, or a Milk Mustache magazine ad. We see and hear them because advertisers pay dearly for them. Conversely, publicity on the same television station or in the same magazine is given freely, at the discretion of the media. They give time and space away because the people who run the station or magazine believe that the story is of interest to their viewers or listeners or readers. Of course, it isn't really free to the client, as he must pay a fee to his public relations agency, which works to drum up media coverage.

At my direction, our PR agency developed a comprehensive—and expensive—event to draw that "free"

publicity. We would take milk away from Californians around the state, including some Hollywood types. After a week, we would interview them and develop stories around their desperate, painful efforts to live without milk. It was true to the deprivation theme. It had broad appeal. It had an edge. It had a lot of things, except, we were soon to discover, news value.

Everything looked fine at the start. A week in April was designated, letters were drafted, participants selected, materials produced. While we weren't able to get any big-name stars, we still believed we had a winner. Costs were beginning to exceed the budget but, with enough coverage, they could be justified. The PR agency began calling the reporters to set up stories and television coverage of "Deprivation Week." Then it happened. Absolutely nothing. No stories. No interviews. No mention of our exquisite milk event. The week came and went to deafening silence. A third of a million dollars had evaporated, and the PR agency didn't seem to have any idea why—not much of an answer.

So I made a telephone call that would prove monumental in the history of GOT MILK? It was to a reporter at a major California TV station, one of the people to whom we had pitched the Deprivation Week story. I called, not out of anger or anguish, but out of interest. Where was our event flawed? Why hadn't she bothered to give it even a mention? Most important, what was she looking for?

The reporter was brutally blunt. Milk Deprivation Week was a fabrication. We had made it up. We knew it.

It was time to launch an aggressive publicity program. It was also time for my "in the box" thinking to trip me up.

She knew it. And apparently, so did every other reporter in California. She was crystal clear about what she wanted: hard, late-breaking news. I was silenced, and embarrassed. It was so incredibly obvious. Infatuated with our own idea, we had not asked the most fundamental, all-important question in marketing: "Who cares?"

Then, this same reporter asked if we were responsible for the new GOT MILK? advertising, for all those hilarious TV commercials and outrageous billboards. Yes, thanks, I replied. Did she really like them? She not only answered yes, she asked a string of questions. Would we be willing to give her the story behind the campaign? Why was it created? Who funded it? Who was the agency? How did we discover milk deprivation? Was there any research? Who came up with GOT MILK? Would

I send her all of our new commercials? Could she run them on her show?

I was eyeball deep in the first of many GOT MILK? interviews. We found our big story because this wonderful woman revealed the secret: the GOT MILK? campaign itself was the interesting, provocative hard news. From that moment forward, we never publicized milk the product, but we sure pitched GOT MILK? the campaign. Over the next six years, it generated more news coverage than any

other campaign in advertising history. It also set a precedent. Nine months later, when the Milk Mustache campaign broke, seemingly in every magazine in America, they wisely leveraged the celebrity ads, not milk, for national publicity.

Not Your Ordinary Campaign

Stories about the campaign surfaced on an almost weekly basis after that, especially in the business press. The flurry of articles was our first indication that GOT MILK? was not your ordinary campaign.

Many of the articles centered on the "Aaron Burr" spot. Journalists were shocked and charmed by a milk commercial that featured an American history buff and a grossly overbuilt peanut butter sandwich. More important, they recognized the truth and power in the concept of milk deprivation. For the first time in memory, the dairy industry wasn't lecturing about the goodness of milk. Here was a campaign that made us want the same white drink we had grown up on by taking it away from us—by putting cookies or peanut butter in our mouths, and cereal in our bowls, and then reminding us that no beverage, not Coke or Snapple or orange juice, could possibly replace milk.

Television news coverage quickly followed, with California stations playing the commercials free within their newscasts, sometimes including two or even three spots in a story. Anchors, reporters, and even weathermen debated the merits of "Baby & Cat" versus "Couple." Initially caught off guard by the coverage, we rallied and fed the media frenzy by sending large quantities of chocolate chip cookies, but no milk, to the stations. Soon, it was commonplace to hear newspeople taunting their cohorts with "GOT MILK?"

We fed the media frenzy by sending large quantities of chocolate chip cookies, but no milk, to the stations.

The campaign had caught fire among California consumers as well. The truth is, they would have had to have been in their bomb shelters (or wine cellars) to have escaped it. Cruising (actually grinding) home from work on the choked freeways, they kept seeing billboards with huge brownies, chocolate chip cookies, gingerbread men, and graham crackers with bites out of them and "GOT MILK?" filling the gaps. If they stopped at the supermarket on the way home, there on the shopping cart, they saw "GOT MILK?" Finally, arriving home and flicking on the TV, they ran directly into the question: "For ten thousand dollars, who shot Alexander Hamilton in that famous duel?"

Luckily for us (and the agency), Californians loved it. Beyond understanding it, beyond laughing at it, beyond recalling it, they gave GOT MILK? the ultimate compliment—they personalized it. They took it to heart and talked about it at home, at the office, at school. One commercial at a time, GOT MILK? began to infiltrate their language and lives. Behavior doesn't change as quickly as the local news, however. We had to wait nearly a year before affection for the campaign made a difference at the dairy case and checkout counter.

Second Phase

Although I can't say we actually knew it then, the campaign was moving into its second phase. (We were working too hard and fast to think about something as cerebral as phases.) The first TV commercials had run at very

high levels, and another pool of GOT MILK? spots was overdue. A series of monstrous questions confronted us. Did we have the creative horsepower to knock out another three or four great spots? Or were "Aaron Burr," "Baby & Cat," and "Couple" flukes? Would my board have the insight and marketing fortitude to take GOT MILK? even further? And would consumers, and the press, continue to embrace this strange "food and no milk" approach?

There was only one way to answer these questions: do the work. Jeff Goodby and I discussed the ground rules over exceptional cups of Berkeley coffee. Yes, we would stay true to milk deprivation. Yes, each GOT MILK? commercial would be a mini-saga, distinct from all others, a tale with a beginning, middle, and end. No, they wouldn't all be set in a kitchen.

We didn't agree on this last point. I felt strongly that a large part of the GOT MILK? magic was its "truism," the fact that almost anyone could relate to the situations we depicted. Goodby, displaying a bit more vision, suggested that by staying in the kitchen, we might begin to trap ourselves creatively. He believed the campaign needed to meander, to seek its own creative high-water mark. He opposed, albeit politely, any immovable creative bounds, as long as we stayed within our deprivation strategy. I reminded myself that he was the creative director (and a very bright man) and I was the client. We could range as widely as he wished, explore even the most bizarre venue, because ultimately the decision, which commercials to produce, fell to the board and me.

Not many weeks later, I was once again sitting across the table listening to GOT MILK? scripts. Scripts that included a cookie catapult, a raging priest, and a case of vehicular manslaughter. This time, the meeting was in my office.

The GOT MILK? "corporate offices" consist of a single 1,100-square-foot room of recycled wood and brick, situated above Bette's, the best diner in the country (or at least in California). We have two full-time employees and one nearly full-time. Every year, we spend about $25 million in advertising, publicity, and promotion. The office is a monument to focus, and I could make a strong case that more good TV commercials have been approved over our seriously

> I was once again listening to got milk? scripts. Scripts that included a cookie catapult, a raging priest, and a case of vehicular manslaughter.

9 STEPS TO FINANCIAL FREEDOM

©1999 T.O. SYLVESTER

Yeah, I got milk. You got money?

selves. They laugh, scream, and, on occasion, storm out of the room. But the ideas keep flowing. And on the day in question in May 1994, we had several logic-bending ideas to discuss.

Castle. This commercial idea has become one of the GOT MILK? standing jokes. It involved a medieval castle under siege. The defenders, led by their stoic king, are fighting a losing battle. But, despite starvation and thirst, they refuse to surrender. The attacking army begins lobbing huge, spherical objects over the castle wall. Soldiers scatter as giant chocolate cookies land in their midst. As they begin gorging themselves, the elated king concludes that the enemy must be cracking. Just then, they look across the battlefield to see the attacking army raise an enormous banner that reads, "GOT MILK?" The king lowers his head and calls for the white flag.

When it was first presented to me in mid-1994, I hated "Castle." I rejected it then and on no less than four

distressed table than in most corporate boardrooms in America. People act like children here. They bungle presentations. They argue and debate. They contradict them-

subsequent occasions. Why? Jon Steel and Jeff Goodby loved it. From my side of the table, it seemed contrived and far-fetched. Castles, kings, and catapult cookies? I didn't buy it. Second, it was too complex. How was a viewer to understand, in 30 seconds, a story that could have formed the basis for a feature film? And finally, what did it have to do with selling milk? It died, along with several others that day.

Vending Machine. A priest sins by stuffing his mouth with devil's food cake—and pays the price. The vending machine won't give up his milk. Desperate, he assaults the machine, only to be caught, face covered in evidence, by two disapproving nuns.

This commercial quickly went into production. The guy we cast for the priest was a wild man. Driven by some hidden rage, he lashed out at the vending machine, mauling it. At one point, without direction, he kicked and smashed the window. We left this scene in the final spot

that began airing in May 1994. And immediately began receiving calls.

As expected, most were from church members. I even spoke to several men of the cloth. All were exceptionally nice, understanding people. I tried to allay their concerns by sharing the results of our research, which indicated that virtually everyone loved the humor in "Vending Machine" and didn't find it offensive in any way.

One caller made a point that was morally irrefutable, however. He reminded me that it was a criminal act to vandalize a vending machine, an act punishable by fine or worse. Unable to argue with that, we went back to the footage, dropped the kick, and put the newly edited commercial back on the airwaves. It turned out to be one of our best remembered and loved spots.

Heaven. An accomplice to murder. According to the script, we were going to run a guy over. The spot opens on a raging type-A businessman striding down a crowded

VENDING MACHINE

VIDEO	**Audio**
OPEN ON FEET OF PRIEST WALKING DOWN LARGE CATHEDRAL HALLWAY.	(MUSIC UNDER THROUGHOUT: CHORAL, HYMNAL CHANTING)
CUT TO REVEAL PRIEST WALKING TOWARD VENDING MACHINE. HE REACHES INTO HIS POCKET FOR SOME CHANGE AND REACHES TOWARD VENDING MACHINE.	
CUT TO CU OF PRIEST'S FACE AS HE SMILES IN ANTICIPATION WHILE SELECTING FOOD ITEM.	
CUT TO PRIEST, POV FROM THE FLOOR DIRECTLY IN FRONT OF HIM, AS HE TURNS AND GRABS CHOCOLATE CAKE OFF PLATE.	
CUT TO CU OF PRIEST STUFFING HIS FACE WITH RICH CHOCOLATE CAKE.	PRIEST:"Mmmmm. Hmmm! Hmmm!
CUT TO POV FROM PRIEST OF CARTON OF MILK BEHIND VENDING MACHINE GLASS ON WHICH THE PRIEST'S FACT REFLECTS.	Mmmmm. Hmmm! Hmmm!
CUT BACK TO CU OF FACE EYEING THE MILK.	Mmmm . . .
CUT TO FULL VIEW OF PRIEST AS HE PUTS CAKE ON TOP OF MACHINE AND REACHES FOR MORE CHANGE.	Mlllkkk!"
CUT TO POV FROM INSIDE VENDING MACHINE COIN SLOT OF PRIEST'S FACE AS A QUARTER DROPS THROUGH THE SLOT.	

VIDEO	**Audio**	

CUT TO CU OF CARTON OF MILK ROTATING SLIGHTLY AND THEN STOPPING.

SFX UNDER THROUGHOUT: STRAINED VENDING MACHINE MOTOR REVVING.

CUT TO CU OF PRIEST AS HE LOOKS AWAY, FRUSTRATED, STILL WITH A MOUTH FULL OF CAKE.

CUT TO POV FROM BACK OF VENDING MACHINE OF PRIEST LOOKING THROUGH GLASS AT CARTON OF MILK SLIDING BACK AND FORTH ON BROKEN ROTATING SHELF. PRIEST KNOCKS ON GLASS.

CUT TO FULL LENGTH SHOT OF PRIEST AS HE TURNS AND LOOKS DOWN BOTH SIDES OF HALL. SUPER: "THE CALIFORNIA FLUID MILK PROCESSOR ADVISORY BOARD." CUT TO CU OF PRIEST'S FACE.

CUT TO POV FROM FLOOR DIRECTLY IN FRONT OF PRIEST AS HE HITS THE MACHINE HARD.

SFX: Slam! (ECHOED)

CUT TO POV FROM BACK OF VENDING MACHINE OF PRIEST THROUGH GLASS AS MILK SLIDES BACK AND FORTH ON BROKEN ROTATING SHELF.

CUT TO FULL LENGTH SHOT OF PRIEST RAPIDLY HITTING MACHINE WITH ALTERNATING HANDS. CUT TO ABOVE VIEW OF HIM HITTING MACHINE.

SFX: Repeated slams (ECHOED).

CUT TO CU OF PRIEST'S PROFILE AS HE LOOKS TO HIS RIGHT. CAMERA PANS LEFT TO REVEAL TWO NUNS STAR-ING AT PRIEST, FROWNING IN ASTONISHMENT.

CUT TO CU OF PRIEST'S FACE AS HE SHEEPISHLY SMILES.

CUT TO TITLE CARD: "GOT MILK?"

VO: Got milk?

city sidewalk. With obvious delight, he fires an underling over his mobile phone. A moment later, he steps into the street and is immediately flattened by a huge truck. The next instant he is being guided into an all-white, ethereal world by an angelic young woman. "Welcome to eternity," she says. Clearly pleased with his fate, and still more than a little cocky, the man spies a plate of "to die for" chocolate chip cookies. He grabs one the size of a discus and takes an enormous bite. "Heaven," he concludes and begins to survey the room. He spies a refrigerator and opens it to find a seemingly endless supply of milk.

Mouth crammed with cookie, he shakes a carton, only to find it empty. He pitches it and tries another. And another. And another. But they're all empty. On his knees and completely broken, he whines, "Wait a minute. Where am I?" The GOT MILK? logo appears on the screen and immediately bursts into flames.

It seemed a bit gruesome to me and I said so. I was assured that it would be done "tastefully." And we had to get him to heaven in order for the spot to work. I relented and agreed to produce it, but only if Jeff Goodby would direct it. He agreed. We shot it and put it on the air in May. *Ad Age* named it the best commercial of 1994. (Torching the GOT MILK? logo was a brilliant touch.)

Creativity Can't Be Taught

This session established the pattern of many to come. My role in the GOT MILK? creative process was a little perverse. One moment I was cultivating, nurturing, protecting, and propagating ideas and creative people. An instant later, I was challenging those same ideas and people; attempting to rip holes in their logic and creativity, trying to raise the creative standard higher, all without pretending that I was any smarter than anyone else in the room. Without intent, I was playing "idea god." In other words, I was being a client.

I was also learning more about the creative process than I had in the prior 25 years in the agency business. At the most basic level, I learned to treasure ideas. I learned to treat each GOT MILK? idea as if it were a gift, something of immense potential value, wrapped in whatever paper the giver had lying around.

GOT MILK? convinced me that creativity can't be taught. It can be encouraged and empowered, recognized and rewarded, but a person either floods the world with ideas or they don't. Few GOT MILK? creative people had classical educations. If they had a master's in this or a doctorate in that, they sure never talked about it. Instead, they spoke in terms of street culture. They knew, or sensed, what was "hot" and what was not—months before the rest of us read it in *Time* magazine. They had a kind of social radar that beeped whenever a mainstreamer like me had an obsolete idea.

Amy is a perfect example of this genre of creatives (in this usage, the word means the people who crank out ad ideas). On the GOT MILK campaign, she worked harder and longer than any sane person I've ever met. Not because Goodby told her to. Not because she was overburdened in her job. Not because she felt threatened. But because she was so intensively creative. If we needed two good ideas, she produced

> **The got milk? creative people had a kind of social radar that beeped whenever a mainstreamer like me had an obsolete idea.**

VIDEO

OPEN ON MAN WALKING DOWN BUSY FINANCIAL DISTRICT SIDEWALK SPEAKING ON CELLULAR PHONE. HE YELLS INTO THE PHONE AND LAUGHS BEFORE WALKING THROUGH A GROUP OF OTHER PEDESTRIANS, KNOCKING OVER AN OLD LADY AND CROSSING THE STREET. HE LOOKS TO HIS LEFT AND THEN HIS RIGHT.

CUT TO SPEEDING TRUCK FROM POV OF MAN. THE TRUCK IS SPEEDING DIRECTLY AT HIM.

CUT TO POV FROM TRUCK OF MAN FROZEN WITH ARMS RAISED, SCARED, LIKE A DEER IN HEADLIGHTS.

CUT TO GRILL OF TRUCK FROM MAN'S POV.

CUT TO BLACK AS DOOR SLOWLY OPENS REVEAL-ING A DREAMY, LIGHT ROOM IN WHICH A CLOUDY IMAGE OF A BEAUTIFUL WOMAN IS SUPER-IMPOSED OVER A WHITE DOVE FLUTTERING.

CUT TO CU OF WOMAN'S HEAD AS IT'S SUPER-IMPOSED OVER WHITE PILLAR AS CAMERA PANS RIGHT TO BEAUTIFUL WHITE ROOM IN WHICH ALMOST EVERYTHING IS LIGHT AND PLEASANT. THE CAMERA PANS DOWN TOWARD A BEAUTIFUL TABLE.

Audio

MAN: (Calmly) "Tom, can I make a suggestion? . . . (Loud) You're fired!!!"

SFX: Truck horn wailing

MAN: "Aaaaaaaah!!!"

SFX: Chimes
SFX: Bird flapping wings

WOMAN: "Welcome to eternity."

VIDEO	Audio
CUT TO CU OF PIANO KEYS. EVEN THE SHARP KEYS ARE WHITE.	MUSIC: Slow, rolling piano intro.
CUT BACK TO ROOM AS CAMERA PANS LEFT TOWARD MAN. IN THE BACKGROUND, THE BEAUTIFUL WOMAN EXITS BEFORE SHUTTING THE DOOR. THE MAN IS LOOKING AROUND. HE LOOKS AT THE DOOR AFTER HEARING IT SHUT. HE'S CAUTIOUSLY CONFUSED.	MUSIC UNDER THROUGHOUT: Slow, easy, swing jazz with alto lead. SFX: Door shutting.
CUT TO HANGING CLOCK WITH NO HANDS.	SFX: Tick, tick, tick.
CUT TO TULIPS AS CAMERA PANS RIGHT. CUT TO WHITE GOLDFISH.	
CUT TO PLATE OF BEAUTIFUL, ENORMOUS CHOCOLATE CHIP COOKIES. AS MAN'S HAND GRABS COOKIE, PAN UP AND PULL IN ON FACE AS MAN BITES COOKIE.	
CUT TO WHITE CAT PURRING BELOW WINDOW.	SFX: Cat purring.
CUT BACK TO MAN CHEWING AND SMILING. HE STARTS LAUGHING WHILE CONTINUING TO INHALE THE COOKIE. HE TURNS.	MAN: "Heaven! . . .

HEAVEN

VIDEO

CUT TO TOP VIEW OF MAN WALKING TOWARD ENORMOUS FRIDGE. HE PULLS DOOR OPEN AND FINDS THE FRIDGE STOCKED TOP TO BOTTOM WITH MILK CARTONS. HE RAISES HIS ARMS AND LOOKS UP JUBILANTLY.

CUT TO STATUE WITH RAISED ARMS IN SIMILAR POSITION.

CUT TO POV FROM BEHIND MAN REACHING TO GRAB A CARTON.

CUT TO FRONT VIEW OF MAN. SIPPING CARTON, AND UPON REALIZING IT'S EMPTY, HE LOOKS IN AND DROPS IT.

CUT TO POV FROM ACROSS TABLE BEHIND MAN REACHING IN FRIDGE.

CUT TO CU OF MAN HOLDING ANOTHER CARTON LOOKING UP, WORRIED.

CUT TO QUICK BODY SHOT OF MAN TOSSING CARTON BEHIND HIM.

CUT TO REAR SHOT OF MAN TOSSING THROUGH MANY EMPTY CARTONS IN SEARCH OF A FULL ONE.

Audio

Yes! . . .

Hmmm . . .

VIDEO	**Audio**

CUT TO HAND TOSSING CARTON STRAIGHT UP ABOVE STATUE.

CUT TO BODY SHOT OF MAN'S HANDS SQUEEZING A CARTON.

CUT TO TOP VIEW OF MAN REACHING TOWARD CARTONS LOADED INSIDE FRIDGE DOOR AND TOSSING THEM OVER HIS SHOULDERS.

CUT TO POV FROM BACK OF FRIDGE OF MAN FRANTICAL-LY GRABBING BUNCHES OF CARTONS.

CUT TO REAR SHOT OF MAN ON HIS KNEES TOSSING MORE CARTONS BEHIND HIM AS THEY BOUNCE AROUND.

Milk!…

CUT TO TOP VIEW OF MAN HUNCHED OVER ON BOTTOM SHELF OF FRIDGE.

Wait a minute. Where am I?"

CUT TO BACK OF SHELF POV OF MAN HOLDING ONE EMPTY CARTON IN EACH HAND. CAMERA ZOOMS IN TOWARDS HEAD BETWEEN CARTONS.

SUPER: "CALIFORNIA FLUID MILK PROCESSOR ADVISORY BOARD."

CUT TO TITLE CARD. "GOT MILK?" SUPER IS SPELLED OUT IN FLAMES ON BLACK.

ANNCR. VO: "Got Milk?"

20. If Goodby or I displayed the slightest hesitation or reservation about an ad, she spent that night reworking it, scrapping it entirely if necessary, and birthing a new and better one for the next day. But it was really after an idea was approved for production that Amy's intensity flamed. She literally devoted her life to the idea. Days, nights, weekends, hotels, airplanes. All became a blur. She embarrassed me with her devotion to my business.

Harry and Sean (other Goodby creatives) were similarly intense, like two creative cannons firing off rounds. They ventured into my Berkeley office with 5 or 6 "official" GOT MILK? ideas, another 10 or 12 stashed like ammunition in an innocuous folder. We usually started with taunting and teasing banter, loosening up before launching into the creative discussion. Did Harry's wardrobe include anything other than white T-shirts? Was Sean, a new dad, sleeping at the office just to get some much-needed rest? Did I catch

Risk both whets and gnaws at the ego.

anything, other than microbrews, on my latest fishing trip with Goodby? They were taking my temperature, getting a sense of my receptivity, and I was trying to give the right signals to communicate that the game was wide open and any idea was welcome.

Before we knew it, we were into the creative session. Harry, a gifted writer, led with a script. Sean, who thought and spoke in pictures, filled in gaps and embellished the idea. We did this two or three times, polite and a bit restrained at first. Then, as if on cue, I challenged them, pushing for bolder ideas. They visibly ignited. Ideas came out of tightly folded scraps of paper. At times Harry wrote them down as he conceived them. The pace quickened. We trashed one idea only to resurrect it in a different form a few minutes later. After half an hour or so of creative crossfire, we took a communal deep breath, retraced our steps, and decided what, if any, commercials to test.

A bull by nature, the GOT MILK? creative process taught me to cultivate risk. Risk is oxygen and adrenaline to the creative mind. It delivers a surge of energy. It sustains maximum effort in the face of exhaustion. It's the springboard for unprecedented performance. And it both whets and gnaws at the ego. People spend their entire lives being told not to take risks. Risk runs counter to stability. It increases the chance of mistakes. It can lead to damage and failure. It is, well, risky. What the world conveniently forgets is that normality is toxic to creativity, and risk is the fuel for anything exceptional.

Risk became so central to GOT MILK? that we now take it for granted. Today, it doesn't seem all that risky to abandon "good for you" and focus instead on milk deprivation. Putting peanut butter or cookies in a guy's mouth and torturing him seems tame and sensible now. Even the decision not to show milk in milk ads doesn't seem all that scary, but when we started the campaign, these moves were considered job-threatening risks. I recall a

board member saying that he thought GOT MILK? was a weird, risky idea, but, what the hell, if it didn't work, they would just fire Manning.

The Movable Deadline

The GOT MILK? campaign also taught me a valuable lesson about deadlines and creativity. Fast-forward to mid-1996, by which time we had produced 18 outdoor billboards. While we had missed the mark on a few occasions (namely a series of distorted food images), most of the work was simple and graphic and dramatized the acute need for milk with core foods. But we needed GOT MILK? outdoor creative to do more. It needed to go beyond getting people to think about milk. It needed to get commuters to stop and buy it on their way home.

The first set of ideas were okay, but just okay. Among them was an octagon, a stop sign. The intended message was "Buy milk now or buy it later," meaning if you don't stop to buy milk now, you or someone else at your house is going to want some later and you're going to have to go out again to get it. While the idea wasn't nearly clear or surprising enough, the sign concept seemed to have value. So rather than scrap it, we decided to turn it on its head, to keep the sign but express it in a completely different way.

Two of our best billboards came out of this reverence for an idea. Both were designed to look exactly like

got milk?

NEXT 1,582,000 EXITS

highway signs with the symbols, displayed from left to right and silhouetted against an official blue background, for a restaurant (a knife and fork), a telephone, and a gallon of milk. Inside the gallon were the inevitable words: "GOT MILK?" The second in the series simply read: "Milk. Next 1,582,000 Exits."

This reverence for ideas, regardless of source and initial appeal, served another subtle but important purpose. It made people working on GOT MILK? feel "safe." And when creative people feel safe, their production, loyalty, and passion explode. The opposite is true as well. When, out of impatience or stupidity, I threatened creative people, their contributions shrank immediately. A creative person is not that different from a hand-shy puppy or child. If you are aggressive, you may get obedience, but never brilliance.

I recall a *New Yorker* cartoon in which two senior executive types are fishing on a lake. One observes dryly

WHILE THE GRIDDLE IS HOT

GOT MILK? deadlines were different from those usually observed in advertising. While we certainly set target dates based on business plans, these dates were pliant and defined by when we had the best creative product. We never missed a GOT MILK? deadline. If an idea wasn't the best we could make it by a given date, we moved the date.

The elusive "Pancake Ad" required six or seven such extensions. The challenge was to create an outdoor billboard that both extended GOT MILK? beyond sweets and cereal and reminded people that drinking milk outside the home wasn't prohibited by law. The resulting design was a sound idea. The original layout (nothing more than a rough drawing in marker pens) was of a stack of pancakes with "GOT MILK?" drawn in syrup on the top.

Right on the money. Pancakes were closely associated with milk; for some people, inedible without milk. The ad moved us beyond the core foods, and pancakes are eaten both at and away from home. And, the use of the syrup writing was unexpected and funny.

Unfortunately, pancakes and syrup are both brown. I noted that I thought legibility was going to be a real challenge (actually, the word I used was "problem"). Both the art director and Jeff Goodby dismissed my concerns. "We'll retouch it," they said (meaning that the people in the photo lab would work some magic). Maybe. I also reminded all the concerned parties that this new billboard was scheduled to post, or go up, in about six weeks. "Not a problem," they said. I was unconvinced, but we went ahead.

The creative team put together a comp, or version of the ad that uses a real photo, in this case, of a stack of pancakes. It wasn't a pretty picture. Yes, the pancakes looked great—fluffy brown and screaming for an ice-cold glass of milk—but the syrup-drawn "GOT MILK?" blended into the pancakes so perfectly as to be invisible. I suggested that they give that retouching guy a ring and get moving.

Weeks passed and we didn't have creative we could run. The photo was retouched and retouched and retouched some more.

The infamous deadline passed, as did the next two. Finally, four months and tens of thousands of dollars after the photo was taken, the ad was clear and readable and appetizing beyond belief. Production of the ad had defined its own deadlines. It also led to a costly charge-off (an expense the agency pays because of a mistake or mismanagement of a client's budget) for the agency. But it was worth it for breaking us out of the kitchen and into other food groups.

that they haven't caught a fish all day. Without missing a beat, his buddy (clearly the executive VP of marketing) chimes in, "Let's fire the agency." The perfect attitude for idea genocide.

I also learned that deadlines can be lethal to creativity. It's inconceivable to imagine business, or life, without deadlines. They are, of course, fundamental to effective time management. But break the word "deadline" into pieces. "Dead." I have a strong hunch that, in the early years, this was meant literally. Miss the agreed-upon time and place, and someone dies. "Line." Again, this was almost certainly a real line, as in "a line in the sand" or "in the line of fire." Both of these words reek of the military and, sure enough, the battleground was the birthplace of the deadline.

I seriously doubt that any great piece of art or architecture, literature, or ad campaign could have resulted from anything less than obsessive parentage.

"I'd Like to Thank the Academy…"

My association with the creative people at Goodby confirmed my experience of 25 years in advertising: Creatives have an insatiable need for recognition. This recognition is more for their ideas than for themselves. Their ideas are like their children, and they want their offspring to be suitably recognized and praised. This is, overall, a good thing. I seriously doubt that any great piece of art or architecture, literature or ad campaign could have resulted from anything less than obsessive parentage.

By mid-1994, the GOT MILK? progeny were not only garnering the recognition of the public and media, they were winning creative awards. The advertising industry sponsors dozens of awards competitions, some local, some national, and a few global. As far as I can tell, their primary reason for existence is to partially compensate advertising people for the ungodly hours and effort they devote to trying to sell someone else's products and services. Since few ad people share in the agency's financial wealth, creative awards help feed voracious, unfulfilled egos. Awards also serve as stepping stones in an advertising career, at least for the writers and art directors.

Given that many highly acclaimed campaigns have failed miserably in the marketplace, I didn't pay much attention to GOT MILK? winning a gold this or a silver that. I had taken an oath to sell more milk, and I wasn't about to get excited by the advertising industry stroking itself.

In July 1994, "Aaron Burr" won the Best in Show in the Clio Awards, the Academy Awards of advertising. The Clios make no pretense of being based on sales or profits or results of any kind. They are purely creative awards, handed out by the industry to the industry for creative excellence (whatever that is). There are dozens of categories, including best campaign, best television, best print, right on down to best bus shelter. Thousands of entries are submitted from around the world and range from unknown, small-budget ads to the mega-campaigns for the likes of Coke, Levis, and Budweiser, the production budgets for which are larger than the annual sales of many businesses. While it is quite prestigious to win any Clio, especially a Gold, winning Best in Show is truly a big deal. It's the industry's way of saying that an ad is so special, so intelligent, so well cast and crafted that it approaches art.

At the time, the significance of the Clio escaped me. Someone at Goodby called to say the Clio folks had notified them that GOT MILK? had won "something." This forewarning was given so the agency and client would be sure to have substantial representation at the awards ceremony. At that point in the campaign, I was so deeply immersed in marketing milk that I just mumbled, "Great. I sure hope they plan to hold the awards on the West Coast. I'm not going to traverse the country just to get a little trophy." As it turned out, the

ceremony was held not only on our side of the world, but in our own backyard: San Francisco. My ill-fitting, rented tuxedo aside, it was a grand night. Most of the San Francisco ad community turned out, and the crowd went appropriately wild when it was announced that a local campaign had won Best in Show.

While I may have been apathetic toward creative awards, winning the Best in Show Clio did change the course of GOT MILK?, Goodby, Silverstein & Partners, and, yes, Michael Bay. The award brought national attention to Goodby and helped transform the agency. Here was a regional ad for an ancient product created by a California agency winning Best in Show over ads by the very best and largest agencies in the world. While Goodby did exemplary work for many clients, GOT MILK? was at the core of their growth. (Not long after the Clio win, GS&P was acquired by Omnicom, one of the foremost communications holding companies in the world.)

"Aaron Burr" also fueled Michael Bay's rise to fame and fortune. Not only did it add luster to his reputation as a commercial director, it helped speed his move into feature films: *Bad Boys, The Rock, Armageddon.* I wonder if, as he directs some Hollywood superstar, he ever thinks back to that funny commercial about Alexander Hamilton, a peanut butter sandwich, and GOT MILK?

Now, in addition to producing fabulous advertising, GS&P began paying a public relations dividend for GOT MILK? The agency was *hot.* Throughout 1994, it won every creative award around, often dominating the competition. It also won new business from some of the monoliths of Madison Avenue, and Jeff Goodby was gaining recognition as one of the country's creative forces. The result was that the agency generated massive coverage, not just in

The strategy of chuckles was beginning to pay off.

the advertising press, but on the business pages. And almost without exception, the coverage linked Goodby, Silverstein & Partners to GOT MILK?

The Clio award also did something for the GOT MILK? campaign that was, at the time, unimaginable. It served as the springboard for the campaign to be licensed nationally. News coverage of the Clios raised our profile among dairymen across the country. Several states (Washington, Idaho, and Oregon) licensed GOT MILK?, and others expressed interest in doing the same.

Finally, California milk sales began to climb. After tumbling two to four percent in the early 1990s, sales were actually up 1% in 1994, the first full GOT MILK? year. Per capita consumption, which had gone steadily down the tubes for 20 years, stabilized at 23 gallons per person. Something was happening to the milk business out West, and the rest of the country was taking note. The strategy of chuckles instead of lectures was beginning to pay off.

Yummy!

ATED

Cookie Dough

18 OZ
9.2 OZ) 510g

got milk?

From Giggles to Guilt

Nothing succeeds, or fails, as conclusively as a joke. That's because humor polarizes people. It makes us either laugh or run for cover. It is self-apparent that humor is one of GOT MILK?'s vital organs. Humor is how got milk? distinguished itself from all past milk advertising and most competitive beverage advertising. Humor is so integral to GOT MILK? that we discard commercial ideas without mercy if the scripts don't generate a laugh.

Of course, we don't always agree on what's funny. Often the folks from the agency are holding their sides after reading a script, while I'm trying to figure out what's so damn amusing. Disagreement is part of the process. Challenging humor elevates it to a higher plane by forcing changes that will make the joke impossible to miss.

got milk? DOES CHRISTMAS

The genesis of this commercial was a remark made in one of our infamous focus groups. One fellow brought up Santa. Gesturing expressively, he asked what would happen if, on Christmas Eve, Santa found a tray of gooey, warm brownies, but no milk? Wouldn't he get just a bit testy? Wouldn't he take revenge in some way? A copywriter on the other side of the mirror noted the remark and, a few months later, we found ourselves getting ready to produce our first GOT MILK? Christmas spot. In it Santa gets his brownies, finds the milk carton empty, and not only takes back the presents, but hauls away the Christmas tree and the living room furniture.

It should have been hilarious. We had a wickedly funny idea, a well-known director, and enough time. But life on the production set isn't always so simple. The first symptom of a problem was with the wardrobe and makeup. Rather than looking like a lovable, classic Santa, the actor walked onto the set looking like he had been in a North Pole barroom brawl. Dirty, disheveled, and more than a little roughed up, his beard was at half-mast and he looked pissed (in both the English and American senses of the word; drunk and angry, respectively).

Enter symptom number two. It appeared that the director and the agency's two creative people had decided that they neither needed nor wanted help from the client, so they evaded and ignored. The next bump came in the form of props. This was a Santa spot. The home was a cozy traditional one with floral wall-

Recently, I was in the office before daybreak, sipping my mandatory double decaf low-fat cap (cappuccino, for the uninitiated), when it struck me that it had been months since I had watched all the got MILK? TV commercials. So out came the historical reel and on went the VCR. With

some painful exceptions, the work still made me smile. Not because we did it but because the ads were funny. I like "funny." Without humor, I'm quite sure that we, as a species, would have become extinct. And without humor, GOT MILK? would have gone away by popular demand.

paper and random-plank hard-wood floors. So what were those naked mannequins doing in the hall? Not only were there complete, anatomically correct men and women, but an assortment of miscellaneous body parts. This took the Hollywood concept of extras just a step too far. Perhaps I could have lived with a messy Santa, but not nudity and body parts. I none-too-gently queried the creative team and director about the mannequins. Mumbles and grumbles, but no real

answers; they were simply someone's exceptionally bad idea. The mannequins disappeared.

The bad news got worse. Santa was directed to be mean to the point of vicious. Too much time was spent on silly, irrelevant action. The "food in the mouth, but no milk" humor of the spot was never captured. When Santa took all the presents back, it was a true act of vengeance and malice and not the least bit funny. In the end, it would have been counterproductive to run the commercial. We had just flushed several hundred thousand dollars down the toilet.

Reviewing our past confirmed for me that GOT MILK? (like all good comedy) is funny because it was born of a basic human truth—in this case, that running out of milk is a pain in the butt. Each 30-second commercial is like an individual episode in a sitcom series: a funny, abbreviated novella with a beginning, middle, and end that capsulizes a broader, cynical take on life.

GOT MILK? humor falls into four basic categories: body laughs, smart laughs, tasty laughs, and emotional laughs.

Body Laughs

The first category is physical, akin to the slapstick in cartoons. Children laugh every time they see muscle-bound Popeye bash Pluto over the head because it's pretend and taps into some primeval funny bone. Similarly, consumers giggle when they see one of

Each 30-second commercial is like an individual episode in a sitcom series that capsulizes a broader, cynical take on life.

our anti-heroes, desperate beyond words, go berserk over his lost milk. What has probably happened to them more than once—an experience they surely didn't find funny at the time—is taken to the hilarious extreme.

Body Cast. Built on the physical, slapstick form of humor, this was one of those spots that was destined to live. From the time it was first presented, there never was a question that it would be produced. A hospital patient, for a reason never revealed, is in a full toe-to-temple body cast. The only visible openings are holes for his eyes and a slash for his mouth. The torture begins as the family visiting the next bed unveils a plate of huge, home-made cookies and a gallon of ice-cold milk. A thoughtful little girl stuffs an entire cookie into the mouth of Mr.

Body Cast. The family happily munches and guzzles as our hero spasms wildly, but hopelessly, for milk.

"Body Cast," which began airing in March 1995, was unusual among our commercials in that we used milk, lots 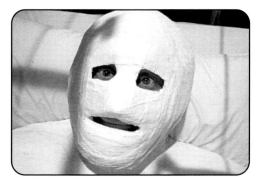 of milk, as a way to contrast and intensify deprivation. The production went relatively smoothly, at least for those of us in the background. For the actor in the body cast, however, it wasn't all that pleasant a day. While the set was a balmy 70 degrees, the temperature inside the body cast was sizzling—well over 90. And once he was locked in, we couldn't release him for hours at a time. We eventually had to cut vents in the cast so as to increase the chances of his living through the shoot. "Body Cast" was definitely one of our sicker ideas. Teens and kids loved it, especially his strangled cry for milk.

Isolation. In this intensively physical, very funny spot, a college student volunteers for a week-long science experiment. He is led around a spacious-looking observation room filled with an assortment of comfy furniture and entertaining goodies—a stereo, VCR, TV, etc. Much to his delight, he discovers an unlimited supply of his favorite cereal. Life is good. He'll kick back for a few days, make a few bucks, and get back to some serious beer drinking and coed chasing.

He is, as always, starving. Having poured an oversize bowl of cereal, he's on the prowl for milk. He opens the fridge, pushes aside the peanut butter, and picks up a half-gallon of lowfat. It is, of course, empty. Very empty. He realizes he's been trapped. A week of cereal but no milk. Beyond desperate, he slams into the one-way mirror. Begging and pleading with his own reflection, he is a

ISOLATION

VIDEO	**Audio**
OPEN ON A SHOT OF TWO SCIENTISTS PLACING PROBES ON A COLLEGE STUDENT WHILE A SCIENTIST IN THE BACKGROUND IS STOCKING THE CUPBOARDS WITH SOMETHING.	AUDIO ANNCR: "Mike Procter is a student
CUT TO CU OF WIRES RUNNING INTO A HEART MONITOR IN THE HANDS OF THE SCIENTIST.	at
CUT TO STUDENT'S FACE SMILING WITH PROBES ON HIS FOREHEAD.	Buckley University,
CUT TO STUDENT PLAYING PINBALL SMILING AS THE SCIENTISTS PREP THE ROOM..	
ZOOM IN ON TWO SCIENTISTS PUTTING CHEERIOS ON A SHELF IN THE KITCHEN.	and he's about to participate in a remarkable experiment. Heading the research effort . . .
CUT TO SCIENTIST WITH LAB COAT, OTHER SCIENTISTS ARE BUSILY WORKING IN THE BACKGROUND. SUPER: *Dr. Iqbal Theba, PhD. Buckley University.*	Dr. Iqbal Theba, Ph.D."
CUT TO SHOT OF STUDENT SITTING IN A LEATHER EASY CHAIR SMILING AS HE RECLINES THE CHAIR & LOOKS DIRECTLY INTO THE CHAIR INTO THE CAMERA GIVING TWO THUMBS UP.	DR.: "Uh, The subject is 24 years old, we are trying to make it very comfortable for him . . .
CUT TO SHOT OF STUDENT LOOKING AT TV PLAYING VIDEO GAMES.	we have big screen television, uh, video games . . .

VIDEO	**Audio**
STUDENT WALKS INTO THE KITCHEN, TAKES A BOX OF CHEERIOS OFF THE SHELF & POURS THE CEREAL INTO A BOWL.	stereo. And of course, plenty, plenty of his favorite food.
CUT TO CU OF SCIENTIST PULLING THE DOOR CLOSED TO THE ROOM.	He will live inside this small chamber.
CUT TO SHOT FROM INSIDE THE FRIDGE. WE SEE A CARTON O MILK AS STUDENT IS REACHING IN FOR IT.	Cut off from all human contact, in the name of science.
HE LEANS CLOSER INTO THE REFRIGERATOR AND POURS THE MILK OVER HIS BOWL OF CHEERIOS. A SMALL AMOUNT OF MILK SPLASHES OUT OF THE EMPTY CARTON.	
CUT TO CU OF LARGE STEAL LOCK ON THE DOOR MOVING INTO PLACE, LOCKING THE STUDENT INTO THE ROOM.	SFX: Milk pouring out of carton, as door locks.
CUT TO THE STUDENT STILL SITTING IN THE FRIDGE AS HE HEARS THE LOCK. HE QUICKLY TURNS TO LOOK THROUGH THE SMALL WINDOW IN THE DOOR AT TWO EYES STARING BACK AT HIM. THE STUDENT IS SHAKING THE EMPTY MILK CARTON BACK AND FORTH. THE SCIENTIST SLIDES A SHADE OVER THE GLASS.	Alone."

VIDEO

CUT TO THE STUDENT STILL SHAKING THE CARTON AS HE GETS A PANICKED LOOK ON HIS FACE AND HEADS BACK TO THE OPEN REFRIGERATOR. BUT THERE IS NO MORE MILK ON THE SHELF. HE KNOCKS JARS, ETC., OVER IN THE FRIDGE.

CUT TO A PAN OF THE ROOM WITH STUDENT RUNNING TOWARD A DOUBLE MIRROR WITH THE EMPTY CARTON STILL IN HIS HAND. HE HITS THE MIRROR WITH HIS HANDS.

CUT TO SHOT WITH CAMERA ON THE OTHER SIDE OF THE MIRROR, STUDENT HAS A PANICKED LOOK ON HIS FACE.

CUT TO STUDENT'S HAND ON THE MIRROR SHADING HIS FACE (HE'S TRYING TO SEE THROUGH THE MIRROR). THE MILK CARTON IS STILL IN HIS HAND. SUPER: CALIFORNIA FLUID MILK PROCESSOR ADVISORY BOARD.

CUT TO THE STUDENT FRANTIC POINTING HIS THUMB BACK TOWARD THE REFRIGERATOR (SHOCKED).

CUT TO STUDENT PACING BACK AND FORTH IN A PANIC.

Audio

STUDENT: "Hey, this one's empty there, 'ya know?"

ANNCR: "For the next 30 days."

STUDENT: "Ahhhhhh. No, no, no, no. I didn't sign on for this. . ."

STUDENT: Guys?

STUDENT: I got tons of cereal . . . (crying)

STUDENT: ok, it's ok, I know you're in there . . .

VIDEO

CUT TO STUDENT STARTING TO CRY AS HE LEANS AGAINST THE GLASS WITH HIS HANDS CLENCHED AND THE PROBE STILL ON HIS FOREHEAD.

CUT TO SHOT OF SCIENTISTS STARING AS ONE HOLDS A CLIPBOARD AND THE OTHER EATS A BIG BOWL OF CHEE-RIOS WITH MILK. BOTH ARE NODDING THEIR HEADS.

CUT TO SHOT OF STUDENT WITH HIS FACE PUSHED UP AGAINST THE GLASS WITH HIS FINGERS PINCHED TOGETHER BEGGING.

CUT TO TITLE CARD: *Got Milk?*

Audio

STUDENT: I want some milk (crying).

STUDENT: ok, it's ok.

Pretty please . . . just a little bit?"

VO: Got Milk?
SFX: Student crying in the background.

notes from the set

Commercial #40: Cooking With Chad

Chad, the sleazy host of a television cooking show, attempts to wow and woo his audience by eating an habañero, the world's hottest pepper. He plans to save himself with a glass of milk, but a thirsty crew member leaves him hot and dry. We had over 100 wax habañeros made for the spot. Chad the actor ate them all. Lucky for him, he didn't have to swallow. (First ran April 1999.)

sad, slobbering, truly desperate sight. We cut to the other side of the mirror to reveal two scientists, both calm and contemplative. One is holding a large bowl of cereal, the milk slopping over the spoon and down his chin. (The dribbling milk happened by accident. Fortunately, the camera caught this perfect touch.) The other says, as dispassionately as if observing an insect, "Interesting." We close on our student, now completely broken, face flattened against the glass, whimpering pitifully for milk.

"Isolation" was a joy to produce. An unexpected yet plausible idea, it is one of our funniest spots due to impeccable casting. In the casting session, after only a few minutes with the script, the actor who played the student delivered a nearly perfect performance. He convinced us that he was the only person on earth who could play the role. On the set, he added to every scene,

> # The campaign treads the line between good and bad taste and, on occasion, steps over it.

improvising lines and creating an entire body language of milk deprivation. He embodied desperation in a most believable way.

The two scientists were also a delight. Understated and completely detached from the student's plight, they are the counterpoint, the contrast that makes viewers laugh every time they see the spot.

Smart Laughs

The second form of humor appeals to the intellect. More subtle than physical humor, it requires a delicate touch, both in the words and visual images of a commercial. While we hope that all GOT MILK? spots are smart, some reach a higher intellectual plane in eliciting laughter. Smart laughs require more from viewers—more attention to the story line, to facial expressions, to the intonations of the actors, even to the music.

notes from the set

Commercial #21: Oreo Kane

This spot spins a fantasy about the naming of the Oreo cookie; based, of course, on milk deprivation. The set, a 1940s corporate board-room in the middle of a Hollywood studio, was very authentic. In answer to the big boss' request for a name for the cookie, a subordinate, his mouth full of Oreos and the pitcher of milk in front of him empty, says, "Arh wo wo" (translation, "I don't know"), and is declared brilliant. I am forever amazed at what "gaffers," the handymen and women of the entertainment business, can create out of scraps of wood, coat hangers, and masking tape. Entire walls are built and destroyed. Large pieces of furniture such as bookshelves materialize within minutes. And an hour after we abandon the set, the boardroom is gone, the commercial palette clean and ready for the next shoot. (First ran April 1996.)

"Santa," with its milk-deprived Claus retreating up the chimney with the Christmas trappings, as well as everything in the living room, is a classic example of smart humor. So is "Interrogation."

Interrogation. In this cerebral spot, which made people both think and laugh, two detectives (who could have come directly off the set of *NYPD Blue*) are unsuccessfully interrogating a slimy-looking suspect. The prisoner fixates on something. The cop asks: "Are you looking at my cupcakes?" He gives the suspect what looks to be a Hostess cupcake. The suspect immediately devours it, his grizzled cheeks bulging. The officer breaks into a knowing smile and places a carton of milk on the investigation table. With absolute confidence, the officer asks: "Do you want to do this the easy way or [dragging the milk out of reach] the hard way?" Case closed.

This commercial was designed so that it would have been virtually impossible to predict what product it was

for or where it might lead. It looked more like programming than advertising. Even after the bite was taken, it would have been tough to guess the turn it would take. Only after we see the carton being removed and hear the punch line do we get it. They've deprived this poor bastard of milk to get a confession. Damn, that was smart.

Two issues that surfaced on the production set suggest how seemingly small things can make or break the humor in a spot. The first sparked a heated discussion between the art director and me. He wanted a dark, dank prison cell in the background. For him, it added credibility to the set. For me, it changed the tone of the room from real to threatening. From smart to scary. The cell went away. The second issue was more lighthearted. On impulse, the detective changed the word "cupcakes" to "Ding Dongs": "Are you looking at my Ding Dongs?" It was hilarious, but we went the cupcake route to avoid a call from the makers of Ding Dongs and possibly their attorney. Looking back, I wish we had taken the risk.

Tasty Laughs
(Laughs on the Good/Bad Taste Line)

The definition of good (or bad) taste is a moving target. It shifts with time, geography, societies, cultures, and individuals. It depends heavily on the source, and on delivery. Two politicians or comedians (sorry, I get them confused) could say exactly the same words and the world would judge one to be revolting and the other hysterically funny. Taste definitely plays a role in the GOT MILK? campaign. We tread the line between good and bad taste and, on occasion, step over it.

Refrigerator Love. We stepped over the good taste line in a little-known spot called "Refrigerator Love." The idea was a spoof of the famous erotic food scene in the movie *Tom Jones.* In the GOT MILK? version, a partially dressed, comical couple seated across from each other begin to feed each other leftover desserts—a handful of cake, a squeeze of éclair, some chocolate frosting here and there. The eating picks up steam, as does the couple. The woman alluringly whispers something in the man's ear. He lights up and races out of the room. We hear a moan of desperation from the kitchen, her face drops, and the magic is irrevocably lost. The screen goes black and up pops "GOT MILK?"

The spot was a struggle from the moment production

Commercial #20: Refrigerator Love. Sparked memories of the movie *Tom Jones.* This spot featured lots of gooey food, lusty lip-licking, soft cooing (all right, moaning), and no milk. By the end of the day, I'm not sure that the actor wasn't taking the romance just a little too seriously. All that foreplay, you know.

Commercial #41: Bones

Our first and only foray into the calcium wars. A mom lectures her son and daughter about the importance of milk for strong bones. They ignore her until their neighbor, who never drinks milk, lifts a wheelbarrow and his arms fall off. We spent over eight painful (boring) hours setting up the arms stunt. In the end, we used low-level explosives to blow his arms off—tastefully, of course. (First ran April 1999.)

INTERROGATION

VIDEO

OPEN INSIDE THE INTERROGATION ROOM OF A POLICE PRECINCT HOUSE. TWO DETECTIVES ARE WITH A SUSPECT. IT LOOKS LIKE THEY'VE BEEN GOING AT IT FOR SOME TIME. IT'S A TENSE SCENE. THE SUSPECT IS SITTING AT THE TABLE. THERE'S A BROWN PAPER SACK, A HALF EATEN SANDWICH AND TWO SNACK-TYPE CHOCOLATE CUPCAKES. SUPER: CALIFORNIA FLUID MILK PROCESSOR ADVISORY BOARD.

WE SEE THE SUSPECT'S FACE. HE LOOKS TIRED BUT DEFIANT AND UNCOOPERATIVE.

THE FIRST DETECTIVE LOOKS AT TOMMY, SEEMS TO NOTICE SOMETHING, LOOKS DOWN AT THE TABLE, THEN AT TOMMY.

WE SEE THE SUSPECT EYEING SOMETHING.

WE SEE THE SUSPECT GRAB ONE OF THE CUPCAKES AND START MUNCHING ON IT. THE SECOND DETECTIVE LOOKS OVER, INTERESTED. THE SUSPECT CHOMPS ON THE CUPCAKE. HE'S GOT A WHOLE MOUTHFUL.

Audio

DET. #1: "All right, Tommy, you're looking at ten to fifteen, why don't you help yourself out?

Are you lookin' at my cupcakes?

Go ahead! Take a bite!

'Attaboy . . .

VIDEO	**Audio**
CUT TO THE FIRST DETECTIVE START TO PULL SOMETHING FROM THE PAPER SACK ON THE TABLE.	All right now . . .
WE SEE THE SUSPECT, STILL EATING THE CUPCAKE. HE LOOKS UP AS HE NOTICES WHAT THE DETECTIVE PULLS OUT OF THE BAG. HIS EYES REGISTER A BIT OF SHOCK AT WHATEVER IT IS.	
CUT TO THE SECOND DETECTIVE SMILING.	. . . we can do this the easy way . . . SFX: sound of something being set on the table.
CUT TO THE FIRST DETECTIVE SLIDING A CARTON OF MILK BACK, AWAY FROM THE SUSPECT, CLOSER TO THE CAMERA.	. . . or we can do it the hard way."
CUT TO THE FACE OF THE SUSPECT. NOW HE LOOKS COMPLETELY DEFEATED.	Suspect: "Gulp."
CUT TO TITLE: GOT MILK?	AVO: Got milk?

began. We argued about the wardrobe. The creative team kept trying to take clothes off. I lobbied to keep them on, lest we X-rate the spot. The food was the next point of difference. The director wanted frosting smeared across most body parts, including legs and chests. I argued that it would be senseless and too explicit. Then came body positions. How about him on top, dropping little morsels of cream into her mouth? By that point, I felt we had lost the humor and crossed into the land of really bad taste. We finished "Refrigerator Love" and showed it to focus groups. Frankly, I didn't care what they said—it wasn't going to run for long. Response to the ad was lukewarm. Predictably, some guys liked it. Most women found it offensive. It ran for a few weeks in April 1996 and was pulled.

Airplane. Sometimes events beyond one's control can transform what people consider funny and in good taste. In spring of 1996, we produced a spot called "Airplane." While founded on milk deprivation, it was about as far from the kitchen as we could get. A commercial airline pilot is handed a cookie by a flight attendant. After a few moments of gluttony, he needs milk. Badly. He turns to see the beverage cart at the rear of the plane. On it is a glistening pitcher of milk. The pilot gets a devilish glimmer in his eye and gently noses the plane down. The cart slowly begins to roll forward, toward the cockpit's open door. It stops, a wheel lodged against a discarded peanut. Frustrated, the pilot takes the plane into a pronounced nose dive. The peanut is crushed. The cart rumbles forward and the pilot, face covered in cookie, gleefully says, "Come to Papa." It's not to be. The door to the restroom swings open. We hear the pitcher shatter as the pilot's face drops.

We were still on the good taste side of the line with this ad, but it started running a week before the ValuJet crash in Florida in May 1996, which killed all 109 people aboard the plane. We never got a call from the public, but the dairy industry chose not to run the spot nationally.

Emotional Laughs

Having watched thousands of people react to GOT MILK?, I am continually struck by the emotional charge in our best work. People of all ages and backgrounds are moved by GOT MILK? Without emotion, humor would be dead. You can't reason people into giggling, just as you can't reason people into consuming more milk. GOT MILK? has mined many emotions, but a few keep surrendering the greatest treasures.

Guilt

I hate guilt. And I'm not all that crazy about people who use it. It always seems to hurt, to tear someone down. This didn't, however, stop us from using it. Guilt is actually one of the primary emotional engines that drives GOT MILK? There's a good business reason for playing on it. If people didn't feel guilty about running out of milk, about not having enough milk for their children's cereal or their spouse's coffee, then depicting the terror of an empty carton wouldn't do much good.

There's more guilt than usual floating around these days. Why? Because working moms are well aware that they're also absentee moms, that they're missing a big chunk of their children's lives. And that their kid's diet is suffering. Moms bolt for the office while their kids are still in bed. They're not around for the after-school snack. And they often "assemble" dinner rather than cook it. Our job was to exaggerate this guilt to the point of silliness, to get people to laugh about how bad they feel when they run out of milk, and to compel them to overstock the refrigerator with fresh milk.

got milk?

Commercial #19: Birthday Party

The world's most inept magician ticks off a party of senior citizens by making their milk disappear. Eight people with an average age of 75, some of whom couldn't hear well, a small space, 14 hours, and a director without patience. A formula for commercial failure. But the seniors were tough and tenacious. The crew helped keep them comfortable (and awake). And the director finally stopped screaming, listened to his crew and actors, and got some convincing performances. (First ran April 1996.)

Two of my favorite billboards fall into the guilt category. One shows an impossibly cute, five-year-old, pink-pajama-clad little girl. She is holding a bowl full of cereal. Dry, crunchy cereal. No milk in sight. Her eyes plead in the way only a little girl's can. The only words, aimed directly at the heart of every parent, are . . . well, you know.

A couple of years later we had an idea that included the world's greatest cookie sellers: Girl Scouts. One has to ask why we stuff our kitchen cabinets with boxes and boxes of Thin Mints each year? Sure they taste great. Sure the money goes to great causes. But the real reason has nothing to do with frostings or fillings. It's because no one with a pulse can say no to those little girls in green. There they stand, award patches adorning their uniform, eyes brimming with expectation. And we place our order. If we didn't, the guilt would take our breath away.

So we asked the Girl Scouts of the USA for permission to use their girls, green uniforms and all, in a GOT MILK? billboard. Because we were a not-for-profit organization and because one can't even think about Thin Mints without milk, they generously agreed. Soon, three heart-melting Girl Scouts were asking motorists across the United States that all-important question.

Vengeance

While psychologists may not consider the desire for vengeance a true emotion, no one seeks revenge in a state of calm objectivity. As most normal folks view the desire for vengeance as an unworthy impulse, how could it help sell milk? The truth is that seeking revenge can be extremely funny. And when used carefully, it can make an incisive point.

Lunchroom. The story was born in truth. A fourth-grade bully is making his usual rounds of the school cafeteria. He swings by a table of innocent-looking girls with the goal of harassing them and, while he's there, picking up a few choice treats from their lunch boxes. This lunch hour, though, the girls are ready. Apparently in fear, they hand over a peanut butter sandwich, cookies, and a cupcake. He greedily stuffs them into his bulging face and looks around for milk. The first carton is empty. So is the second. He turns to a little girl with a big thermos, certain that he's found the mother lode of milk. She grudgingly

NASTY CALLS FROM DISGRUNTLED VIEWERS

There's a narrow path to tread in all comedy. Veer too far to the left and you're up to your navel in bad taste and bad press. Swing too far to the right and the "goody, goody" boredom buzzer goes off. You won't get complaints because no one will notice.

My preference is to tick off only a few people and entertain the rest. In other words, if we don't get a few disgruntled calls from people who take issue with our spots, I'm disappointed and a little worried. Here are two typical examples of fallout from our not playing it safe.

Aaron Burr

Many people, from advertising experts to the Fed Ex delivery guy, have called "Aaron Burr" the nearly perfect commercial. It was surprising and funny, well cast and acted, on-strategy and beautifully produced. It entertained people and sold milk. It also bothered a few folks.

What were the complaints about? The fact that we depicted someone talking with a mouth crammed with food. I mean, you could actually see the glob of partially chewed peanut butter when he screams "Aaaawon Buuuhhh" into the phone. My answer was simple: it was funny and, if he hadn't had his face stuffed with food, he wouldn't have needed milk. At the same time, I apologized for offending anyone.

hands it over and shoots a knowing glance at her table mates. His confidence fully restored, he throws back his head, tilts the thermos, and opens his mouth. He's rewarded with a fluttering piece of lined paper with the words "GOT MILK?" The girls erupt in laughter and the thermos heroine closes the spot with a classic raspberry.

Santa

The calls on Santa caught me off guard. Most complained that we were taking liberties with a religious, or at least sacred, figure. Most were concerned with the effect on children. As a result of the latter, we modified the scheduling so the Santa spot would run only after 9 P.M. That seemed a reasonable compromise.

Then he called. He never gave his name. Instead, he opened the call with an angry barrage. How dare we make his five-year-old son cry? Who did we think we were, showing Santa taking away all the presents, along with the Christmas tree and furniture? This guy was really mad (literally?) and all I could do was listen until the fire died down. When he had cooled a bit, I apologized if our commercial had upset his son and rather innocently asked when he and his son had seen the spot.

Without hesitation, he replied that it was about ten in the evening, during *NYPD Blue*. Father to father, I asked him what was a five-year-old doing up that late and why was he watching a finely produced, but clearly adult show. Now I was on the offensive and it had to do with parenting, not TV commercials. My caller immediately backtracked and soon sought a reason to disengage. Before he did, I strongly suggested that reading his child a Berenstain Bears story at 8 P.M. might be a good next step.

It's worth mentioning that when this ad ran in May 1997, it was the first time that the words "GOT MILK?" were an integral part of a commercial story, versus a tag or signature line. It reflected the growing penetration of "GOT MILK?" into the American vernacular. It was evolving from a popular ad slogan into an everyday figure of speech.

Paws. We've even used feline vengeance. In this spot, a grandmotherly type runs out of milk for her herd of cats and, sensing crisis, attempts to substitute nondairy creamer. The ploy fails completely. Purring turns to snarling. Kitty revenge begins. The "beasts" close in on her. The spot ends as a somewhat menacing paw hits the breaker switch.

This shot proved that we could stretch milk deprivation

beyond "food in the mouth, no milk." Producing it reminded me, however, why smart people avoid working with too many animals and too many animal trainers. We used five or six cat trainers (kitty wranglers) and 25 or 30 cats. We were assured that, despite all knowledge to the contrary, these cats would do almost anything we asked of them. Instead, they acted just like cats and did exactly what they pleased. The shoot took from 6 A.M. to 1 A.M. the next morning. We ended up using fake cat paws for most of the close-ups, including the breaker switch shot.

Desperation

Desperation is the emotional core of GOT MILK? We've portrayed characters so intensely desperate for milk that their very survival seems to hinge upon getting one long, cool mouthful.

Hall of Mirrors. Set in a carnival, this commercial depicts such a man. A hammy clown who is also a glutton has just downed a monstrous powdered doughnut, but he has misplaced his milk. He reaches for the carton, only to bump his head on a mirror. He sees it again, but again it is only an illusion. Growing more crazed by the second, he spins to see giant milk cartons reflected to eternity in the mirrors. (Okay, we took some creative liberties.) Finally, convinced that he's identified the real carton, he races headlong into the camera. We cut to "GOT MILK?,"

hear a loud thump, and return to watch him slowly peel off his own powdery reflection.

The mirrors in this spot proved to be a menace. It was core to the story that the milk carton be projected on five or six mirrors, seeming to surround our desperate victim. Easy to say, hard to do. Every time we got the carton perfectly focused on one mirror, it was bent and contorted on another. Or the mirror picked up the image of a camera or a cameraman. The crew solved the problem after several hours of their own agonizing desperation, and the spot went on the air as planned in August 1998.

Animal Crackers. One of our most complex and emotional spots, this is a story of total desperation. A story where someone's survival actually depends on milk—spilled milk. The commercial was produced in conjunction with Digital Domain, the animators who gave us *Titanic*, and it features both live action and computer animation.

ANIMAL CRACKERS

VIDEO	Audio
MS OF LITTLE GIRL AT THE KITCHEN COUNTER POURING THE LAST OF THE MILK INTO A GLASS. CAMERA PULLS BACK TO REVEAL FRAME OF COOKIE BOX WINDOW FROM THE COOKIES' POV.	MUSIC: twinkly, happy RHINO: "uh-oh . . ."
CUT TO CU OF A BOX OF ANIMAL CRACKERS SITTING ON THE COUNTER. WE SEE THEM THROUGH THE CELLOPHANE WINDOW ON THE FRONT OF THE BOX AS THE SHADOW OF THE GIRL'S APPROACHING HAND FALLS OVER THE BOX.	RHINO: (Nervously, to the other cookies): "We got trouble."
CUT TO ECU OF THE LITTLE GIRL'S HAND ENTERING THE BOX OF COOKIES FROM THE COOKIES' POV.	MONKEY: (Softly praying that he won't be selected by the little girl) "Oh, please not me."
CUT TO CU OF THE LITTLE GIRL EATING A HANDFUL OF COOKIES.	SFX: Crunching. MUSIC: Suddenly darker. ALL: (Reacting in horror to the girl eating) "Owww! Ahhhh! Ewww!"
CUT TO CU OF THE COOKIES IN THE BOX.	RHINO: (Shocked as if witnessing a horrific car wreck): "That's gotta hurt!"
CUT TO CU OF THE LITTLE GIRL AS SHE SETS DOWN THE GLASS OF MILK AND LEAVES THE ROOM.	MOM: (Calling from another room) "Tracy!"
CUT TO ECU OF THE COOKIES IN THE BOX.	ELEPHANT: (To the other cookies) "We gotta do somethin'!"
CUT TO A SNAP ZOOM OF GLASS OF MILK.	MUSIC: Dramatic ELEPHANT: (Gasp!)
CUT TO MS OF COOKIES JUMPING THROUGH THE CELLOPHANE WINDOW ONTO THE COUNTER TOP. SNAP ZOOM INTO ELEPHANT AS HE POINTS THE WAY WITH HIS TRUNK.	SFX: Rip. ELEPHANT: "Chaaaarrrrge!"
CUT TO WS OF COOKIES STAMPEDING TOWARD THE MILK AS THE CAMERA BOOMS DOWN.	ALL: (Stampede sounds)

VIDEO	Audio
CUT TO WS OF COOKIES PUSHING THE GLASS.	ALL: (Straining to push the glass): "Uuughhh!"
CUT TO WS OF GLASS TIPPING AND SPILLING TOWARDS CAMERA.	ELEPHANT: "Timber!!"
CUT TO WS OF LITTLE GIRL RETURNING IN THE DISTANCE AS THE SHEEP POPS UP IN THE FOREGROUND.	SHEEP: (Sees the little girl returning): "She's ba-a-a-a-ck!" ELEPHANT: (Directing everyone back into the box) "Let's go!"
CUT TO MS OF COOKIES JUMPING BACK INTO THE BOX.	RHINO: (Noticing that the Monkey's the last man out) "Run Monkey, run!"
CUT TO MS OF MONKEY STILL RUNNING TOWARD THE BOX. THE MONKEY TRIPS AND FALLS.	MONKEY: (Falling behind, panicking): "I'm not going to make it!" MUSIC: Dramatic climax.
CUT TO CU OF COOKIES IN THE BOX.	RHINO: (Hushed, to the other cookies) "She's gonna to eat Monkey!" ALL: Whispers. MUSIC: Tentative, suspenseful
CUT TO MS OF LITTLE GIRL EXAMINING THE SPILLED GLASS OF MILK AS SHE HOLDS THE MONKEY COOKIE IN HER OTHER HAND.	SFX: Drip ELEPHANT: "Not without milk."
CUT TO WS OF LITTLE GIRL YELLING FOR HER MOTHER, THROWING THE COOKIE BACK, AND LEAVING THE ROOM AS THE CAMERA BOOMS UP. *LEGAL SUPER*: CALIFORNIA FLUID MILK PROCESSOR BOARD.	LITTLE GIRL: "Mom!" MUSIC: Playful resolution.
TITLE CARD: "GOT MILK?"	ANNOUNCER? VO: "Got Milk?"
CUT TO WS OF COOKIE BOX. THE MONKEY JUMPS BACK INTO THE BOX AS THE OTHER COOKIES CELEBRATE.	MONKEY: "Who's the monkey now?" ALL: (Celebrating, laughter) "Yay!"

The spot opens as a box of animal crackers is being invaded by a giant human hand (actually, it belongs to a seven-year-old girl). After munching down several crackers, the giant is called away by her mother. Led by a heroic elephant, the desperate animal crackers break out of the box and tip over the girl's glass of milk. Hearing her return, they race back to the shelter of their box. All but one. Monkey trips, falls, and is grabbed by the girl. Just as she prepares to decapitate him, she notices that her milk has been spilled. Confused and angry, she throws Monkey down and stomps out. Victorious, the animal crackers have survived another day.

The challenge was to infuse the animal crackers with humanity so their desperate plight would be personalized by viewers. This was accomplished not only through their appearance and movement, but by giving them distinct and appealing personalities. Elephant moves and speaks like the intelligent leader. Kangaroo is the never-say-die soldier. And Monkey is the near victim of his own goodness.

• • •

A final note on humor. Advertisers and viewers make an unspoken deal. We put the ads in front of them, and they choose whether or not to pay attention. If a GOT

MILK? commercial is interesting, entertaining, informative, valuable in some way, maybe they'll pay attention. Maybe they'll even consider buying and drinking more milk. If GOT MILK? doesn't provide anything of worth, however, then it will be ignored—as the vast majority of television advertising is. In my clearly biased opinion, humor is the best currency advertisers have.

People attach value to humor. If we can get them to smile, or better yet laugh out loud, they'll give us their attention. And maybe even some of their milk money. A word of caution, however: Irrelevant humor, along with irrelevant sex and violence, may attract, but it doesn't persuade. In fact, it may backfire as intelligent consumers recognize and resent the irrelevance.

got milk?

From Ad to Icon

People had definitely started giving us both their attention and their milk money. With milk sales showing an increase in 1994, we started 1995 feeling very sure of ourselves. But despite some wonderful creative work, as the months passed, we saw that it was not shaping up to be a great sales year. Questions about milk deprivation were being raised by the board and me, and we had not yet licensed the campaign nationally. The Milk Mustache program was being tested, and it focused squarely on "good for you."

Following a presentation of several new GOT MILK? television scripts to the board, one member asked why we weren't giving consumers hard, tangible reasons for drinking more milk—such as calcium, protein, vitamin D. Why weren't we telling people what was good about milk, rather than just reminding them that it's a pain to run out? Also, wasn't GOT MILK? getting tired? How long could we keep saying the same thing? Good questions, tough questions.

This meeting was an illustration of a maxim that should go in fortune cookies. We get bored with our

It struck me that I had badly mismanaged the expectations of my board.

stocks, our jobs, and our ad campaigns about a week before they start paying big dividends. In our case, GOT MILK? had been running in California for nearly two years, and some board members were getting a bit bored. They never actually said the word, but these questions were sure signs and symptoms.

I was caught off guard, as were the folks from Goodby. There was silence. In those few moments, it struck me that I had badly mismanaged the expectations of my board. Rather than leaping into yet another round of GOT MILK? television commercials, we should have discussed what the campaign could, and couldn't, be expected to produce. And how quickly. We should have taken the time to remind the board, which was composed of men whose lives revolved around milk production rather than commercial production, why milk deprivation was still so

right, why it still held such unbounded potential. We should have played videotapes from focus groups in which consumers not only recalled the story lines of GOT MILK? commercials, but recited them verbatim.

The moment passed, and I thanked the board member for his questions and laid out the logic of our path. The board quickly restated their support for GOT MILK?, and we moved on through a long agenda. No one realized how close we had come to losing the campaign's direction. A few months later, GOT MILK? was licensed nationally and began its upward trajectory into icon status.

Going National

The move toward becoming a household word, so to speak, began with a call I will never forget—from Tom Gallagher, CEO of Dairy Management, Inc. (DMI). DMI had only recently been created to represent dairy producers or farmers nationally. Their milk marketing program was in flux; they weren't thrilled with their ad campaign or the agency behind it. Against all odds, Tom suggested that they might be interested in licensing the GOT MILK? campaign from us. A national group licensing an entire campaign from a state organization was unheard of. And milk producers and processors were traditionally enemies, not allies. (Producers want prices high. Processors, the folks who buy the milk, want them low.) These two groups joining together to sell more milk may seem an obvious strategy, but it was actually a novel concept in the milk industry.

I said we were interested. Very interested. Very definitely interested. Here was a possibility for GOT MILK? to attract, provoke, and engage on a completely new and national scale. Maybe, just maybe, it might sell more milk. And yes, it crossed my mind that we could generate a few pennies in licensing revenues in the process.

We never lobbied to license GOT MILK? to DMI. If we had, the partnership probably would not have been consummated. Instead, a political war would likely have broken out in which GOT MILK? would have been judged, and, I believe, sacrificed. We would have been caught in the political crossfire between processors and producers,

national groups and California, and various ad agencies. By refusing to engage in politics and by staying focused on great advertising creative, we allowed the decision about the value of the GOT MILK? campaign to be made in the marketplace.

A presentation here, a huddled lunch there, dozens of well-placed phone calls by the right people to the right people and, by October 1995, GOT MILK? was playing on television screens in virtually every home in America. Less than two years later, national awareness of GOT MILK? would be over 80 percent and pushing 90 percent among teens.

> Here was a possibility for got milk? to attract, provoke, and engage on a completely new and national scale.

Calling All Rabbits

Meanwhile, I had placed another call that transformed GOT MILK? from an ad campaign into a property, from a

California tag line into a national icon. To area code 612. Minneapolis—home to General Mills and Pillsbury, cereal and cookies, the Trix Rabbit and the Doughboy. Arguably the most important city in America to the milk industry. I dialed from home at 6:30 A.M. Minneapolis is two hours ahead. Years of chasing East Coast people had taught me a critical lesson: Ring before their day gets rolling, before their defenses are up. My objective was simple: open the door to cross promotions between General Mills' cereal brands and California milk.

The early morning trick worked. I reached a woman in the promotions department. She, of course, had no idea what the California Milk Processor Board was. Nor did she recognize my name or "GOT MILK?" Unsolicited business calls are tough—I had about ten seconds to snare her interest. But I had three strong cards to play.

First, I gently reminded her that General Mills' brands were highly dependent upon milk. Not much cereal is consumed with soda or OJ. Second, I stated that we were committed to helping them sell more cereal in California. And lastly, I casually mentioned that we had a $25 million budget.

Her response was complete silence. It was too much for a promotions manager to "digest." On the other end of the line was some crazy guy from the California milk industry with a multimillion-dollar budget offering to help sell their brands of cereal. I knew we were making progress when she asked, "*Who* are you and *what* is your budget?" Unrestrained enthusiasm followed. Of course milk was crucial to them. Of course they wanted to

National awareness of got milk? would grow to be over 80 percent and pushing 90 percent among teens.

become promotion partners. Of course they would design California-specific promotions. Of course they would give away coupons for milk. Of course they would put "GOT MILK?" on their display materials, maybe even their cereal packages. It was just that no one from the dairy industry had ever called before.

General Mills became our first and most prolific promotion partner. Over the next three years, we worked with their brands more than a dozen times. They put "GOT MILK?" on millions of boxes of Cheerios. They offered GOT MILK? T-shirts on the side panels of their cereal boxes. They dropped hundreds of thousands of coupons offering free milk to Californians. And we helped them sell cereal in every way we could, from covering some of their promotion costs to running GOT MILK? ads featuring their brands.

With General Mills as a template, the GOT MILK? promotions program exploded. We went on to forge promotions alliances with Kraft, Pillsbury, Kelloggs, Quaker

Oats, Nabisco, Entenmanns, Keebler, Nestle, and Dole. These companies have sold massive quantities of cereal, cookies, peanut butter, and so on in California and have given away millions of gallons of milk. The result was a "win-win-win-win." Consumers, retailers, food companies, and the milk industry all gained. And we all became just a little bit more codependent. Not surprisingly, the California program broke ground for food and milk promotions on the national front.

Dole

One of our least predictable partnerships was with Dole. What does a company trading in pineapples and bananas have to do with milk? The answer is in the cereal bowl. More bananas are used on cereal than any other fresh fruit. (Number one overall is raisins.)

Due to a serious case of marketing obsession, I routinely do store checks; that is, I voluntarily walk around grocery stores and observe how people shop, what they buy, what they pick up and don't buy, the routes they take through the store, their reaction (or lack of reaction) to special displays and promotions, their interaction with their kids and employees, and, of course, what happens in the dairy department.

On one of these store checks, I happened into the produce department. As always, there was a sizable mound of bananas on display, and each cluster had little Dole stickers on them. Bananas go on cereal. Milk goes on cereal. Bananas carry stickers. "GOT MILK?" fits on a sticker. How about putting GOT MILK? stickers on Dole bananas? In two weeks, we were in a promotions partnership, and several months later,

GOT MILK? stickers appeared on 100 million clusters of bananas across America. Dole and GOT MILK? received national press coverage because the partnership had set a marketing precedent (this was in fall 1997). Suddenly, fresh fruit became an advertising vehicle, and stickers popped up all over the produce department.

Trix

The most important reason for the success of the GOT MILK? promotions program was that we put our partners' needs first. It may seem counterintuitive to do this, but it made sense because the companies whose needs we were considering brought invaluable assets to the table. And this approach was crucial in getting the companies that made brands such as Trix and Oreos and Rice Krispies to allow us to use their icons in our advertising. Icons that had required decades of effort and hundreds of millions of dollars (perhaps billions in the case of Oreos) to build. Take the Trix/GOT MILK? commercial, which started run-

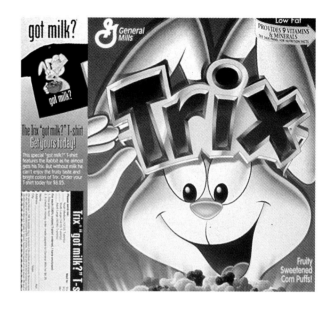

ning in California in April 1995, and then nationally in June.

This spot was a direct outgrowth of the increasing trust between us and General Mills. We were deep into a new round of GOT MILK? creative development and were struggling to come up with a truly surprising commercial using cold cereal. We chose cereal since it represented about 25 percent of milk consumption—consumption we couldn't afford to lose and weren't likely to pick up later in the day. We were struggling because our "Couple" commercial had been built around cereal and was proving tough to beat creatively.

The breakthrough came when we decided to explore cereal icons, not just generic cereal, or even brands. The result was a script unlike anything we had seen before. It would require a new level of cooperation from General Mills—not just from their promotions people, but from their top management.

Trix Are for Kids. The script tells the story of a somewhat disheveled young man who, apparently late at night, seems to be stalking the cereal aisle of a convenience store. He picks up three cereal boxes, including Trix. The checkout lady, no mainstream character herself, laughs eerily and says, "Trix are for kids." The youth runs home, locks the five or six dead bolts on his front door, and lunges for the kitchen table, already set with the requisite

bowl, spoon, and milk. Crazed, he pours nearly the entire box of Trix into the bowl.

He then begins to unzip his head. Yes. He reaches back and unzips a perfect body mask, while crowing, "Finally, after all these years of 'Trix are for kids.' Well now they're for rabbits." As the mask is removed, none other than the Trix Rabbit is revealed. He has finally come up with an infallible

scheme to get his Trix. It looks as though years of desperation and failed plots have come to an end. He reaches for the carton of milk and pours, eyes flashing success. But the carton is empty, save for a few pitiful

TRIX

VIDEO

OPEN ON A CU SHOT OF A PAIR OF MAN'S SNEAK-ERS ENTERING THE STORE.

CUT TO THE WOMAN AT THE REGISTER LOOKING AT HER TABLOID MAGAZINE. SHE TURNS TO THE GUY AS HE SETS THE CEREAL BOXES DOWN ON THE COUNTER. SHE PICKS UP THE TRIX BOX. THE GUY LOOKS AT HER NERVOUSLY.

CUT TO MED SHOT OF THE GUY'S FACE. HE LOOKS DOOMED.

CUT BACK TO THE WOMAN. LAUGHING, SHE TURNS TOWARD THE REGISTER TO RING UP THE GUY'S CEREAL.

CUT TO A SHOT OF THE GUY ENTERING HIS APARTMENT.

CUT TO THE GUY, HIS BACK UP AGAINST THE DOOR, STILL CLUTCHING HIS CEREAL. HE LOOKS TO THE LEFT.

CUT TO CU OF HIS FACE AS HE LOOKS RIGHT.

THE GUY RUSHES FROM THE DOOR, DROPPING THE CHEERIOS AND WHEATIES BOXES.

CUT TO A FULL SHOT OF THE GUY AT THE TABLE, OPENING THE BOX OF TRIX.

Audio

SFX: Suspense music builds in background.

SFX: Box being set on counter.
WOMAN: (Puzzled) "Trix? . . .

SFX: Doors slamming shut.

. . . Trix are for kids. Ha, ha, ha, ha, ha, ha . . ."

SFX: Door opening.

SFX: Slight SFX of guy's back hitting the door.

SFX: Fallen boxes hitting the floor.

VIDEO	Audio
CUT TO A SHOT OF THE GUY SITTING DOWN AT THE TABLE, GRASPING THE TRIX BOX. HE POURS THE CEREAL OUT OF THE BOX INTO THE BOWL.	SFX: Guy collapsing in chair. GUY: "Finally, after all these years of . . .
CUT TO ECU OF TRIX BEING POURED INTO THE BOWL. SUPER: SPONSORED BY THE CALIFORNIA MILK PROCESSOR BOARD.	
CUT TO A SHOT OF THE OVERFLOWING BOWL OF CEREAL AS THE GUY KEEPS ON FILLING IT WITH TRIX. WE SEE THE TOP OF THE GUY'S HEAD FROM ABOVE THE BOWL.	SFX: Sound of cereal hitting the bowl. . . . Trix are for kids!
CUT TO THE ALMOST MANIC LOOKING GUY SETTING THE TRIX BOX DOWN, REACHING BEHIND HIS HEAD, UNZIPPING HIS HEAD.	GUY: Well . . . SFX: Zipping.
CUT TO CU OF THE GUY AS HE UNZIPS HIS FACE. HIS EYES FOLLOW THE ZIPPER AS HE ZIPS DOWN.	Today . . .
CUT TO THE GUY'S "BODY" FALLING TO EITHER SIDE AS THE EXUBERANT TRIX RABBIT EMERGES FROM HIS "DISGUISE." THE JOYOUS RABBIT GRABS THE MILK CARTON AND STARTS TO POUR IT OUT OVER THE BOWL. ONLY A SPLASH OF MILK COMES OUT.	TRIX RABBIT VO: . . .they're for . . . Rabbits!!!" (Cackling laughter follows) SFX: Pathetic splash.
CUT TO MED SHOT OF THE UNBELIEVING, CRESTFALLEN RABBIT AS HE LOOKS AT THE EMPTY CARTON IN HIS HAND.	AVO: Got milk?

drops. His face literally collapses as he realizes that it isn't going to work. Then, and only then, do the words "GOT MILK?" pop up and we understand why his quest was doomed from the start.

Imagine going to General Mills with this script. We wanted to "borrow" not only their brand and icon, but also their almost universally recognized tag line: "Trix are for kids." This was forging new territory in our promotions partnership. In addition, we were proposing that Goodby, an agency that General Mills had absolutely no connection with, produce the spot. Despite these potential obstacles, the spot was enthusiastically embraced because we put the Trix brand first. We involved their people from the onset. We used their TV production consultants and animators. Their folks were at every key meeting and part of all major casting and production decisions. They attended the shoot and participated in the editing process. And we happily put millions of dollars in media behind the commercial and never asked them for a penny.

We made their brand the hero and sold milk in the wake of its success.

Pillsbury

We also had our rejections. Having already successfully worked with Pillsbury on a number of promotions, we approached them with what we believed was a sensational advertising idea. It was a script about a family, a happy family, a Pillsbury sort of family.

The Doughboy. In the script, the mom has just made chocolate chip cookies. Everyone is munching away contentedly. The Pillsbury Doughboy is being his usual perfect self, cooing "Nothing says lov'n like something from the oven." Dad innocently asks for some milk. The son goes to the refrigerator and then informs the family that someone, not him, has put the milk carton back empty. Sister cries innocence. Dad shrugs an "I didn't do it" shrug. Mom, the interrogator, searches the room for the culprit.

The tone of the commercial changes. The Doughboy looks guilty, mumbles "uh oh," and starts to search for cover. The entire family freezes him with their glares. Could he have committed the sin of milk sins? The Doughboy dashes for the exit with the family, faces full of cookies, in hot pursuit. The last thing we see is "GOT MILK?"

The spot added a new facet to the Doughboy's character. He became more human, more vulnerable. The script was a favorite in focus groups. We were prepared to fund the commercial production as well as the television time. Some Pillsbury people loved it—and some didn't. Unfortunately for us, the ones who didn't had bigger titles than the ones who did. They felt that suggesting that the Doughboy would "steal" the last of the milk would jeopardize his credibility and perhaps detract from his enormous appeal. So, while we continued to run cooperative promotions over the years, the Doughboy/GOT MILK? spot never saw the light of the TV screen.

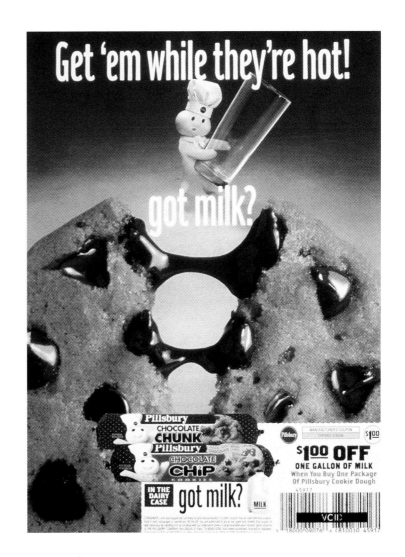

Kellogg

Working with Kellogg's Rice Krispies provided an extra angle to our "food and no milk" theme. Not only can't you eat the brand without milk, you can't even hear it. Without milk, the underpinnings of Snap! Crackle! &

Pop! collapse. Conversely, Kellogg, and its great cereal brands, are crucial to milk consumption.

We had an idea for an outdoor billboard that involved Snap! Crackle! & Pop! We sought to portray these three characters, normally the happiest little guys on earth, as dismayed, distracted, and distressed. Why? Because they had run out of milk for that great big bowl of dry cereal. No hard-sell proposition. No hype. Only the words—you guessed it—"GOT MILK?"

Much to our delight, Kellogg bought the idea without hesitation. We were off and running. But almost immediately we realized that, rightfully, Kellogg was enormously protective of Snap! Crackle! & Pop. Obsessive parents, really. They had invested untold amounts of money, time, and intellectual energy to build this cornerstone brand. Further, they had never, at least to my knowledge, allowed any other marketer to use the characters. They insisted that we use their illustrators and work within their stringent graphic guidelines. This

was an anomaly for us. We're pretty obsessive ourselves about who creates GOT MILK? advertising.

There was a moment when we could have lost this magical partnership. We could have jumped in and passed judgment on each character's expression, attempted to mold them to exactly what we had envisioned—more depressed, more pained, more desperate. But I recalled how incredibly blessed we were. Here was Kellogg, a huge and powerful player in the food industry, allowing us, this little milk board, to use Snap! Crackle! & Pop in our advertising. I shut my mouth and told myself that the creative people would find some workable compromise. To Kellogg's credit, the billboard turned out to be one of the

most popular, and I believe effective, that we've ever produced. And Kellogg remains a valued marketing partner.

No, Thank You

One of the most difficult parts of the GOT MILK? marketing process has been to say no. This sounds more like dating advice than business acumen. They're not all that different. My goal was to capitalize on the power of other brands and icons without making costly, irrevocable mistakes. At times saying no was effortless. Other times, the temptation to "just try it once" was immense.

Over the past five years, we've been fortunate enough to have hundreds of potential partners and projects involving GOT MILK? Many, such as the use of Cookie Monster, Oreos, and the Girl Scouts, just made sense and didn't require any debate. At the opposite end of the spectrum, we've quickly passed on partners and opportunities that were simply "misfits."

For example, we said "no thanks" to an offer to place a GOT MILK? billboard in a Hollywood thriller. At first glance, it looked appealing. Lots of free exposure and press. Upon review of the script, however, we discovered that the billboard (three kittens looking longingly for milk) would be a backdrop for a scene overflowing with graphic violence and bloody animal parts. Not a good idea.

But the toughest "no" decisions were those that involved potentially huge ideas with great partners. For example, Disney approached us with the movie *Hercules*. Their idea was for us to create, in tandem with their world-class illustrators, a GOT MILK? commercial using Hercules and the bad guys. The draw was that the soon-to-be-released movie would be launched with a massive promotional blitz. It would also give us the opportunity to partner with Disney. We tried. We really did. But no matter what angle we took, no matter how we twisted and turned the idea, there simply wasn't a logical link or creative bridge between Hercules and GOT MILK? We said a reluctant "no, thank you."

Barbie Starts an Avalanche

In the early days of our co-branding partnerships, in September 1995, to be precise, I got another stunning telephone call. This one from Barbie. Not the doll, but the brand manager at Mattel. I genuinely thought she had the wrong number. I mean, why would Mattel call us? It turned out that Mattel was about to introduce

a new "Cookies and Milk Barbie," complete with bovine apparel and the classic recipe for Nestle's chocolate chip cookies. It was to be a national Toys R Us exclusive. She asked simply: "Would you mind if we rename her 'GOT MILK? Barbie'?" Mind? I breathed deeply, swallowed hard, pretended that this sort of once-in-a-lifetime offer came daily, and said: "No, go right ahead."

In the next instant, I almost blew the deal. Having tasted licensing blood, royalties flashed across my mind. At even a few cents per doll, this deal could generate money. I am thankful that the words never made it from my bubbling mind to my babbling lips. I'm quite sure

that if, at this early stage in GOT MILK?'s brand development, I had suggested royalties, the deal would have evaporated. So, no money changed hands, and GOT MILK? Barbie was born. And, according to Mattel, she sold very well.

After we hung up, I shook my head. Mattel, not some unknown rag manufacturer, but Mattel, was going to put our trademark on Barbie. We were in the licensing business for real.

Prime Property

As an ad agency guy, I had never had anything to license. Products and trademarks belonged to clients. We simply created campaigns, which also belonged to clients. With no experience in the world of licensing, I soon realized we needed help to navigate its piranha-infested waters.

Toward the end of 1995, I began the search for a licensing agent. It turned out that licensing agents, at least the ones I met (and the two I hired, then fired), are genetically linked to used-car salesmen. They all had 25 years in the business (although one or two couldn't have been over 40). They all had personal contacts at the largest retailers. They all were positive that GOT MILK? gear would soon be knocking Nike and B.U.M. off the shelves. They all promised that royalties would flow like a river in flood stage. And they all were full of themselves and not much more. In the end, their big promises were only big piles. When they didn't lie outright, they stretched the truth beyond recognition. These guys (they were all guys) weren't unlikable. Some were sincere, well spoken, and credible on the surface. They were just hollow. Rather like a book with a provocative title, a terrific jacket, and 200 blank pages.

Despite the players, the GOT MILK? licensing program quickly accelerated. People began to recognize, some before I did, that GOT MILK? had the potential to be a property. Maybe not on the scale of Lion King, but certainly beyond the range of any previous ad campaign. We then made a series of licensing deals that proved these folks right. A designer came to us with the idea for GOT MILK? infant and toddler T-shirts and rompers—packaged in milk cartons. An infant feeding and accessory company proposed a full line of GOT MILK? products. Mattel came back to us with the idea for GOT MILK? Hot Wheels.

Leigh Rubin, creator of the syndicated cartoon *Rubes*, wanted to do a line of T-shirts. Eventually we licensed GOT MILK? for teen and adult apparel, watches, plush animals, luggage, jewelry, and golf balls. We even came close to doing a deal with Joe Boxer for a provocative line of GOT MILK? underwear and sleepwear but, as sometimes happens, the deal fell through. GOT MILK? could only stretch so far.

GOT RIPPED OFF?

Owning a valuable intellectual property is not dissimilar to owning a valuable chunk of real estate. If not carefully patrolled, trespassers and poachers soon begin to steal bits and pieces. I awoke one morning to find that "GOT MILK?" had become fair game for a string of advertisers and their agencies.

My first reaction was sue, sue, sue. Who were these people? What right did they have to steal our trademark? A few had called. But most simply scribbled Got This? or Got That? and ran it.

After a few minutes and a couple of cups of coffee, however, I could see that most of these derivations were so silly, so irrelevant, so far removed from GOT MILK? that people would laugh at them, not with them. The other conclusion, and this was borne out by research, was that these rip-offs actually accelerated the rate at which GOT MILK? became part of everyone's vocabulary. They were helping GOT MILK? to take its place in America's consciousness.

In a few cases, we went after the violator. If we felt something degraded milk or our trademark, we fired off a cease-and-desist letter. Most companies cooperated and pulled the ad. If that didn't work, we pursued serious legal action or, if it wasn't worth the cost and effort, moved on to more critical fronts.

Gotmilk.com

Licensing GOT MILK? led us to our website. Maybe it was my tendency toward counterculture, or the fact that I was computer illiterate, but I strongly resisted birthing a GOT MILK? website. Websites were popping up like some kind of unmanageable mold. Every business *had* to have one. Well, we didn't. What purpose would it serve? We had massive awareness. People loved the advertising. We had great promotion partners. The press loved us. Milk sales were stabilizing,

got jazz?
got brains?
got credit?
got dirt?
got work?
got bait?
got surf?
got hair?
got financing?
got insurance?
got bones?
got fuel?
got balls?
got wine?
got the munchies?
got jesus?
got money?
got change?
got y2k?
got teeth?
got media?
got booze?
got silicone?
got martini?
got math?
got music?
got chocolate?
got beer?
got glasses?
got mud?
got marketing?
got options?
got pride?

maybe even beginning to edge upwards. What exactly was the business objective for a website? One certainly couldn't buy milk there.

But one could buy GOT MILK? stuff there. We had 25 or 30 licensed products, and they were selling. Our problem was that GOT MILK? products didn't have broad distribution. There was, I believed, pent-up demand for our products, especially those aimed at infants and toddlers, but consumers couldn't find them. Gotmilk.com suddenly made sense. An E-commerce site where people could play a "food and no milk" game, learn the history of the campaign, challenge themselves on the GOT MILK? trivia game, and, most important, buy the stuff they couldn't find anywhere else. On October 1, 1998, six weeks after we came to that conclusion, the site was launched. It may even pay out some day. In the meantime, there are thousands of kids running around in GOT MILK? rompers and a few duffers teeing off with our golf balls.

Habla got milk?

Fast-forward to June 1999. The front page of the *Wall Street Journal*, one of the most discriminating publications in the world, carried a story about the California Milk Processor Board. It even included pictures of some balding, bearded guy (me) with two lovely Hispanic marketing women. The reporter related how this commodity board out of Berkeley, California, had spent several months crafting and re-crafting a strategy to influence bicultural Latino teens. The result was that, for the first time, English-language advertising (our GOT MILK? spots) was going to run on Spanish-language TV. My board was thrilled by the strategy and the media coverage. (Their only regret was that a drawing of a milk carton hadn't run in place of my photo in the newspaper.) The strategy of publicizing GOT MILK? the campaign, not milk the beverage, was still paying huge dividends.

got milk? **Does Tinseltown**

The extent to which GOT MILK? had taken its place in popular culture became apparent in mid-1995. A friend called one morning to ask if I had seen the previous night's episode of the Cybill Shepherd show. No, I hadn't. Why? It seems Cybill had done a GOT MILK? skit. In the show, she was left hanging from a crane when the crew took a break for lunch. Cybill, who had no food other than a cupcake, called for help but to no avail. Stuck, she took a bite of the cupcake and asked, "GOT MILK?" When I saw a tape of the show, I thought Cybill had never looked as beautiful or sexy as when she spoke those famous words. Why did she do the skit? She was doing what good comedians are paid to do: spot what's current and use it while it's hot.

Cybill's skit was the first of many onscreen (television and film) cameos by GOT MILK? Today the GOT

MILK? "Tinseltown Tape" is 30 minutes long and has many of the best comedians in the business asking "GOT MILK?"—Frasier, Rosie O'Donnell, Cosby (three times), Jay Leno. GOT MILK? references also appeared on the TV shows *Jeopardy, Mad About You, Party of Five,* and *Friends* and in the movie *As Good As It Gets.* The staying power of the GOT MILK? campaign is evidenced by the fact that the tape is not a finished product but continues to grow in length as fresh segments appear and are added.

If we had tried to produce GOT MILK? skits using some of the biggest names in television, the cost would have been enormous, even by soft drink and beer advertising standards. And even if we had been able to get the capital, the venture would never have gotten past the proposal stage. These celebrities, and their producers, wouldn't have allowed an advertiser to dictate their routines. Hollywood embraced GOT MILK? not because we paid them but because it made their audiences laugh. Every time someone asks if I saw GOT MILK? on this show or in that movie, I'm reminded that really good ideas are their own best sales agents.

When Jeff Goodby tossed off the words "GOT MILK?," no one could have imagined that someday dozens of celebrities would do their own GOT MILK? skits. Or that those words would be attached to Cheerios, Cookie Monster, Oreos, and Barbie. Or that people would visit gotmilk.com to buy hats, T-shirts, dolls, and baby rompers. Hell, all Goodby wanted to do was fill space on a presentation board and win the milk business. As for me, I was happy to have a tag line that a three-year-old could remember.

When I see got milk? on this show or in that movie, I'm reminded that really good ideas are their own best sales agents.

got milk?

chapter 7

Underage Drinking, or Children As Marketing Targets

fall 1994—another got milk? focus group. Behind the one-way mirror again. More of the same salty snacks and M&Ms, interspersed with gallons of bottled water and Diet Coke. Many of the same players shared the dark, stuffy, now familiar room, but a different game was being played. It was three in the afternoon instead of the usual eight at night. The moderator, a young, buoyant woman of 25, was sitting on the floor with a variety of pillows strewn about. But what particularly distinguished this focus group was the drinkers. They were three to four feet tall, couldn't sit still for more than a few seconds, and blew milk bubbles with their straws. GOT MILK? was talking with kids.

Between the bubbles and the babbling, the children revealed secrets. Milk was good for them? How many times had they heard that? The mere mention of calcium had them rolling their eyes. The longer the discussion of milk's nutritional value went on, the more distant the kids became.

Yet prior to the GOT MILK? campaign, the dairy industry had presented milk as a cold, white medicine, a beverage to be administered by parents. From an early age, children hear, "If you don't drink your milk, you won't get

The mere mention of calcium had kids rolling their eyes.

any dessert." While threats and blackmail got milk down the kids' throats, they unexpectedly opened the door for more fun and exciting beverages to steal our kids' business—drinks that are far sweeter than milk, a highly attractive trait to humans, seemingly from birth.

As with adults, the food and milk link was indelible for kids. Once they were past the baby-bottle stage, their milk consumption was driven by certain foods. In specific instances, milk was irreplaceable. Not even soft drinks worked in the cereal bowl or for dunking cookies or with pancakes and syrup. These kids told us that milk occupied an almost sacred role when paired with these foods.

Despite not being shoppers, running out of milk was a disaster for kids. It was also a battleground between those who shopped and those who ate. One particularly lyrical girl told of the morning her mom did the "empty-carton shake." She and her brother had poured their respective cereals, sliced bananas on one, added raisins to the other. They were ready for milk. Mom found that hubby had downed the last of the milk the evening before. It seemed he was addicted to munching graham crackers while watching professional wrestling. She shook the carton, then peered into the mouth as if expecting a miracle. Nothing but drops.

Scrambling, Mom offered bagels. Reject. How about whole-wheat toast? Reject. Maybe some plain yogurt with granola sprinkles? Reject. They didn't want something else. They wanted milk. Dad was in deep trouble. And destined to visit the grocery store on his way home.

Again, as with adults, the need for milk changed as soon as the kids walked out the front door. Once in a fast-food restaurant, a fried drumstick or french fry in their

got milk?

greasy little paws, they became soda freaks. Milk was history. Even in schools, where milk was mandatory on lunch trays, it took a backseat to sugared drinks.

A Marketing Face-Lift

We knew that no group of consumers has less money and more purchasing power than kids. They may have only small change in their piggy banks, but they account for billions of dollars in sales annually. Clothes. Toys. Bicycles. Snowboards. Books. Videos. Games. Foods. Software. Beverages. And, of course, milk. Never in the history of consumerism have more kids had more influence over more money. Today's kids are also the most media-saturated generation on record. They seem to live their life in front of screens: TV screens, computer screens, video game screens, and, of course, movie screens.

Our first job was to give milk a marketing face-lift. We had two choices: Design a separate campaign for kids, or allow kids to discover the GOT MILK? advertising that their parents and older siblings were watching. We chose the latter, not because we were so smart, but because it was a lot more expedient than creating kid-specific commercials. The result was a marketing windfall. Kids found GOT MILK? on their own and fell in love with it. It didn't lecture. Or preach. Or patronize. Or pretend. Or deceive. It didn't do a lot of things that repel media-astute kids.

Instead, it treated children as an intelligent life form. It told the truth. It engaged them. And it got them to say "GOT MILK?" every time someone opened up a pack of Oreos or a box of Cocoa Puffs at the kitchen table. But mostly it got them to laugh. They laughed at the deprivation and desperation of GOT MILK? And their laughter bonded them not only to the campaign but to the beverage.

A got milk? script that girls found adorable, boys found gross.

GOT MILK? also gave them a new vocabulary for milk. Months after a TV commercial had been off the air, five- and six-year-olds could recite, almost word-for-word, the "Aaron Burr" and "Baby & Cat" spots. Kids not only liked GOT MILK? ads, they absorbed them. One mom told us that her daughter had begun asking for a glass of "GOT MILK?"

A Moving Target

But marketing milk to children was tricky, very tricky. Our target was about as far from static as one can get—the rate and magnitude of change in children is astounding. To make it even more fun, kids don't change at the same pace. An advertising idea one five-year-old thought hysterical completely eluded another. And then there's the boy/girl thing. By five or six, they're not only different genders, they're different species. A GOT MILK? script that

FULL BODY CAST

VIDEO	Audio
OPEN ON A HOSPITAL ROOM. WE SEE A FAMILY VISITING DAD AND NEXT TO HIM, IN ANOTHER BED, A GUY IN A FULL BODY CAST.	SFX: Soothing music in background. Muffled hospital SFX. DAD: "Hey! Cookies!"
CUT TO A FULL SHOT OF THE FAMILY ENJOYING THE CHOCOLATE CHIP COOKIES THAT MOM AND THE GIRLS BROUGHT FOR DAD.	DAD: (Gesturing to the guy next to him) "So, you know, I think
CUT TO CU OF THE GUY'S FACE IN THE CAST. HE HAS TWO HOLES FOR HIS EYES AND A SLIT FOR HIS MOUTH. HIS EYES WIDEN IN ANTICIPATION.	our neighbor might like one." GUY IN CAST VO: "Hmmmph?"
CUT TO AN OVERHEAD SHOT OF THE PLATE OF COOKIES. A HAND REACHES IN AND GRABS ONE.	
CUT TO A SHOT OF DAD GESTURING FOR HIS DAUGHTER TO TAKE THE COOKIE OVER TO THE GUY IN THE FULL BODY CAST.	DAD: (Prompting) "Uh-huh, well . . ."
CUT TO A SHOT, POV FROM THE GUY'S EYE HOLES. WE SEE THE GIRL LOWERING THE COOKIE TOWARDS HIS MOUTH SLIT.	SFX: Breathing. GIRL VO: "Here you go." GUY IN CAST VO: "Mmmmm . . . mmmm . . . mmmmm . . .
CUT TO FULL SHOT OF THE GUY'S HEAD AS THE GIRL STUFFS THE COOKIE INTO HIS MOUTH.	(muffled) thank you."
CUT BACK TO POV FROM THE GUY'S EYE HOLES. WE SEE THE GIRL RETREAT.	
CUT BACK TO THE GUY'S HEAD. WE CAN SEE HIM CHOMPING ON THE COOKIE.	SFX: Chomping, crunching. GUY IN CAST VO: (Happy) "Mmm . . . hmmmm . . . mmm . . ."
CUT BACK TO POV FROM THE EYE HOLES. THE CAST MOVES AS THE GUY CHOMPS.	SFX: Chomping, crunching suddenly stops and becomes a choking sound as the guy realizes that he desperately needs something to drink.
CUT TO RACK FOCUS LONG SHOT OF THE GUY'S BIG TOE THAT POKES OUT OF HIS CAST AS WE SEE HIM LYING ON THE BED.	
CUT TO A SHOT OF THE GUY'S HEAD. HIS EYES ARE OPEN WIDE IN TERROR. HE LOOKS TO THE LEFT AS HE HEARS SOMETHING FROM THE FAMILY'S DIRECTION.	SFX: Pouring milk.

VIDEO	Audio
CUT TO A SHOT OF DAD POURING A BIG GLASS OF COLD MILK WITH A COOKIE IN HIS OTHER HAND.	DAD: "Terrific!"
CUT BACK TO THE GUY IN THE CAST AS HE MUMBLES DESPERATELY, TRYING TO GET THE FAMILY'S ATTENTION.	GUY IN CAST VO: (Mumbled) "Ummmmmm . . . 'scuse me . . .
CUT TO A SHOT OF MOM'S HAND AS SHE REACHES IN FOR THE OVERFLOWING GLASS OF MILK.	. . . scuse me . . . people . . ."
CUT TO A SHOT OF THE FAMILY, POV FROM THE GUY'S EYE HOLES.	SFX: Muffled sounds of desperation from the guy in the cast throughout.
CUT TO AN ECU OF MOM'S HAND WITH THE GLASS OF MILK. HER HAND MOVES OFF CAMERA TO REVEAL THE DESPERATE GUY IN THE CAST.	
SUPER: SPONSORED BY AMERICA'S DAIRY FARMERS.	
CUT BACK TO THE FAMILY DRINKING MILK, POV FROM THE EYE HOLES.	
QUICK CUT OF THE GUY'S HEAD AS HE SHAKES BACK AND FORTH.	SFX: Bed squeaking.
QUICK CUT TO DAD AS HE'S GULPING MILK.	SFX: Gulp.
QUICK CUT TO A PULLEY ON THE GUY'S BED SHAKING AS THE GUY THRASHES AS BEST HE CAN IN HIS FULL BODY CAST.	
CUT TO A LONG SHOT OF THE GUY SHAKING IN HIS BED.	
CUT TO THE TWO GIRLS GULPING MILK. WE SEE THE GUY IN HIS BED IN THE BACKGROUND.	SFX: Gulping.
CUT TO AN ECU OF THE GUY'S EYES, OPEN EVEN WIDER IN DESPERATION AND TERROR.	GUY IN CAST VO: "Aaaaaaagh!"
CUT TO THE TITLE: GOT MILK?	AVO: Got milk?

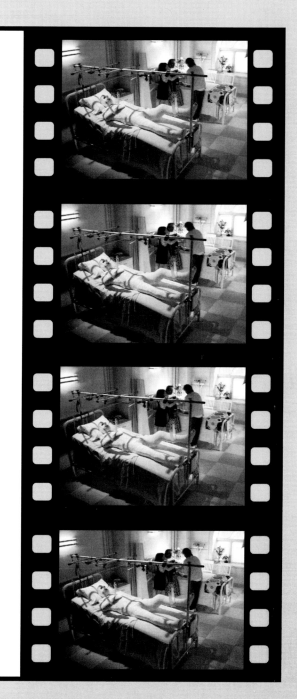

girls found adorable, boys found gross. And a spot that boys judged super cool revolted girls. Mass marketing, a fundamental principle for those who sell brands, fell apart with kids. There is no average seven-year-old.

To compound the confusion, kids don't purchase milk. Little boys and girls don't decide whether to buy one or two gallons or select skim versus 2%. So, as milk mar-keters we needed to create both kid demand and parental compliance. One had to ask (or whine or demand); the other had to pay.

Sponges and Mirrors

In our relentless battle to defend milk consumption by kids, we looked at how these little people think and feel

and what seems to influence their behavior. We concluded that children, especially those under eight, are at once sponges and mirrors. They don't receive input so much as absorb and reflect it. The line between fact and fiction, real and pretend, is blurry at best. Every parent knows when they've made a mistake, when they've allowed a young child to view something that is just a bit too real. Their little fingernails dig into your arm, their body becomes rigid, their breathing gets short, and they are disturbingly quiet. It is clear that they've stepped over the line. Whatever is happening in that scene is real, and no amount of parental persuasion to the contrary is going to change that.

We also noticed that kids don't make much of a distinction between TV programming and advertising. It is all entertainment, filled with heroic, high-flying characters, menacing bad guys, and fantastic, faraway places. The situation is getting even more complex as hit movies, theme parks, TV programs, audiocassettes, dolls, games, clothing, toy stores, fast-food meals, and advertising are being woven into a tightly knit marketing fabric.

Marketing to kids proved to be a painful and costly lesson in tinkering.

Competitive beverage advertising aimed at children drives what is affectionately called the "gimmes" or the "wanta, wanta, wantas." In case you've not recently raised a child, the primary symptom of these dreaded social behaviors is a nonstop, mind-draining series of requests for a product, such as a soft drink or other heavily sugared beverage. Children's thirst for these drinks seems insatiable, and buying the product doesn't quench their desire, it seems to feed it. The more the kid sees soda advertising, the more the kid wants. And the more the kid

Script: Stick Figures

For this commercial, we imported a German illustrator and began a painful animation process, painful because there wasn't enough time and nobody was willing to admit it. Things started smoothly with a discussion of which foods we were going to use, how the stick figures would move across the screen, how they'd develop cavernous mouths, and how they'd be transformed by what they ate. The situation rapidly deteriorated, however. Calls weren't returned. Meetings were canceled. Changes I asked for weren't made. Changes I hadn't asked for were made. Budgets were ignored. A downward spiral had begun.

wants, the more the kid gets. And the more the kid gets, the more the kid wants. Advertising may not have been solely responsible for this syndrome, but it sure jump-started it.

In an attempt to break the "gimme" cycle of kids wanting heavily sugared drinks and to strengthen milk's position with younger members of a household, we reversed our earlier decision not to market specifically to kids. In October 1995, we developed a mini-campaign for kids ages 6 to 11.

It proved to be a painful and costly lesson in tinkering. We knew kids loved the core GOT MILK? campaign, the gooey food, the stuffed mouths, the extreme desperation

of the milk-deprived characters—they told us so every time we asked them in focus groups. We didn't listen and, on my flawed direction, developed a kids' campaign.

"Stick Figures"

The first ad for kids involved animated stick figures that engulfed monster-size foods. Once they snared and swallowed the food, they were reshaped in its image. The results were stick figures in the shape of doughnuts, cereal boxes, and peanut butter sandwiches. When the ads were tested among young children, they understood the concept and seemed to be drawn to the commercials. So far, so good.

Once produced, however, "Stick Figures" didn't resonate with kids. They understood some of the spots (they should always understand all of the spots). They even "kinda liked" them. But they remained cool toward the advertising. It was as if these gluttonous, animated little stick creatures never became real for the children. The figures' quest for milk remained just that, *their* quest for milk. Not that of the kids.

"WHAT DO YOU SAY TO MRS. WILSON, DENNIS?"

"GOT MILK?"

"Stick Figures" was a major write-off for the agency—and us—as in, monetary loss. The creative team that worked on "Stick Figures" departed for another agency. The ads were pulled, and we returned to core GOT MILK? work.

Treating Kids As People

Two years later, in September 1997, one of the national dairy groups, DMI, asked us to develop a GOT MILK? campaign aimed at children. Given our previous experience, we naturally had serious reservations. But it was their money, so we gave it a try.

The first thing research uncovered was that while kids treasured traditional GOT MILK? advertising, they didn't "own" it. It was really funny milk advertising, but it wasn't *their* milk advertising. This shouldn't have surprised anyone. We created the work with teens and adults in mind. Additionally, even though most of the material was

VIDEO

OPEN ON GRADE SCHOOL LUNCHROOM.

CUT TO TABLE OF FOUR SECOND-GRADE GIRLS EATING HOMEMADE SANDWICHES FROM LUNCHBOXES.

CUT TO ONE OF THE GIRLS.

CUT TO DOORWAY. A FOURTH GRADER SWAGGERS INTO THE ROOM. HE'S KIND OF A LARRY MONDELLO-TYPE (THE BEAV'S FRIEND FROM LEAVE IT TO BEAVER), KIND OF A WISEGUY.

CUT TO BOY WALKING UP TO THE TABLE OF GIRLS. HE GRABS ONE OF THEIR LUNCHBOXES AND BEGINS TO RIFLE THROUGH IT.

CUT TO BOY. HE TAKES HOMEMADE CHOCOLATE CHIP COOKIES OUT OF ONE LUNCHBOX.

CUT TO GIRLS WATCHING.

CUT TO BOY AS HE STUFFS COOKIES INTO HIS MOUTH. SLOWLY, HE WORKS HIS WAY DOWN THE TABLE, TAKING ALL THE "GOOD STUFF" FROM EACH OF THE GIRL'S LUNCHES: A PB&J, AN OATMEAL COOKIE, A BROWNIE. HE TAKES BITES OUT OF EACH ONE AND PACKS IT ALL INTO HIS CHEEKS, SMILING.

CUT TO GIRLS, SITTING QUIETLY.

CUT TO BOY. HE FINDS A HUGE TWISTY CHOCOLATE-COVERED DONUT IN ONE OF THE LUNCHBOXES.

CUT TO BOY EATING THE WHOLE DONUT IN THREE BITES.

Audio

SFX: Lunchroom door opens

GIRL: "There he is! He's coming!"

BOY: "So, what did mommy make us for lunch today?"

VIDEO	**Audio**
CUT TO CU OF BOY, HIS MOUTH COMPLETELY STUFFED WITH FOOD, LOOKING AROUND FOR SOMETHING TO WASH IT DOWN WITH.	BOY: "And gnow fo a wittle mook."
CUT TO BOY AS HE GRABS A THERMOS SITTING ON THE TABLE IN FRONT OF HIM. HE SPINS THE LID OFF A THERMOS AND TIPS IT TO HIS MOUTH. IT'S EMPTY.	
CUT TO THE KIDS AROUND THE TABLE. THEY EXCHANGING GLANCES.	
CUT TO BOY. HE GRABS ANOTHER THERMOS. IT'S EMPTY, TOO. HE WORKS HIS WAY THROUGH THE THERMOSES.	
CUT TO A LITTLE BLONDE GIRL AT THE END OF THE TABLE, CLUTCHING HER THERMOS PROTECTIVELY.	
CUT TO THE BIG KID. HE LOOKS AROUND FRANTICALLY. JUST THEN, HE NOTICES THE LITTLE GIRL. THIS, HE THINKS, IS WHERE HE'LL FIND THE MILK.	BIG KID: "Mook."
CUT TO GIRL. SHE HOLDS HER THERMOS TIGHTER.	
CUT TO BOY, WHO COOLLY TAKES THERMOS AWAY FROM HER.	
CUT TO CU OF BOY AS HE PUTS THERMOS UP TO HIS MOUTH, SMILING AT THE GIRL AS HE WATCHES HER OVER THE TOP OF THE THERMOS. HE TIPS IT FURTHER.	
CUT TO A SMALL SLIP OF PAPER FALLING OUT OF THERMOS.	
CUT TO CU OF PAPER AS IT DRIFTS TO THE TABLE. IT HAS "GOT MILK?" WRITTEN ON IT.	
CUT TO CU OF BOY. HE LOOKS UP, PANICKED.	
CUT TO LITTLE GIRL. SHE STICKS HER TONGUE OUT AT HIM.	GIRLS: Laugh

in reasonably good taste, it would never have gotten past children's network censors.

Virtually none of the kid advertising on the air treated children as the savvy, thoughtful little critters they are. It depended heavily on mindless, cutesy characters or random, abstract images. And, of course, there was the ever present "kid music." Very few commercials told a story or attempted to connect with children on their terms, rather than on the advertising agency's terms. It was as if advertisers were afraid to ask kids to think. Maybe they thought the kids would turn in terror. They were, of course, 100 percent wrong.

got milk?

This wasn't a case of us knowing better or of us stroking ourselves by disparaging other people's work. When we showed children samples of advertising directed at kids, they condemned it. The ads didn't make any sense to them, didn't touch them emotionally, or (sin of sins) it patronized them. Based on our admittedly small sample, we found much of the kid advertising was not only a waste of money, it was repelling the very audience it was attempting to attract.

So we wrote a creative brief (background paper) that assumed that children had well-developed brains and were as cynical of bad advertising as their elders. (Teens can raise cynicism to an art form.) We knew that GOT MILK? commercials couldn't "make" kids drink more milk. Rather, the advertising needed to recast milk as a beverage that they could choose of their own accord. Not simply doses of white medicine delivered by their moms. We

Kids feed on the moment, and their favorite food is fun.

also wanted our advertising to live happily within the larger world of milk deprivation. Truthfully, we weren't sure we could pull it off.

Before exploring the creative concepts that were developed, tested, and ultimately produced, let's remind ourselves of how children, say four- to eight-year-olds, come at life. And let's assume (and pray) that they are reasonably well fed, have at least one loving parent, and are as normal as kids can be.

Kids feed on the moment, and their favorite food is fun. Pure, unrestrained, undigested fun. Kids are as much like smart puppies as diminutive adults. They are extremely fragile. They believe that they are the center of the universe (a belief that I happily embrace and promote). As a result, "mine" is an impossibly important concept, a concept closely linked to their self-esteem. Unfortunately, the world rapidly polarizes kids into believing that they are either vital (a truism) or worthless. We wanted our advertising, in its own little way, to promote the former and dispel the latter.

"Backwards World"

We explored a range of creative approaches. One of the most appealing was called "Backwards World." In this commercial (which at this point was nothing more than words scribbled on paper), everything happens in reverse. Kids float out of their kitchen chairs and back into bed. Cats jump backwards off a table onto the floor. Scrambled eggs retreat from the frying pan and become whole again. Cereal

We loved "Backwards World." It was funny. It was intelligent. And it put kids to sleep.

repours (I made up this word) itself into its box. And, of course, milk magically flows out of bowls and glasses and back into cartons, leaving kids high and dry. We loved "Backwards World." It was funny. It was intelligent. And it put kids to sleep. They didn't hate it as much as dismiss it.

Initially, they liked the idea. The problem was that the concept (like so much advertising) was predictable. Kids quickly worked out the backwards model and easily predicted where commercials were going and how they would end. Like successful video games, our kid advertising needed to be more challenging, engaging, and surprising.

About this time, pure creativity came into play. What I mean is that one of the creative teams had an idea that wasn't based on research or even personal experience. It was a pure and simple idea that swelled up from wherever ideas swell up from. The thought was to have kids write their own GOT MILK? TV commercials. We would give them some broad guidelines, but the commercial

ideas would come from their own heads. From their own experience of milk and milk deprivation. They would become our creative directors. We got some local primary-school teachers to allow us to use their students as creative guinea pigs. We sent off several leading questions: "What would the world be like without milk?" and "Who might steal the last of the milk?" Then we crossed our fingers.

The results were startling. We received dozens of ideas, ranging from blatant remakes of existing GOT MILK? spots to incomprehensible concepts to simply dumb ideas. Many of the concepts made no sense or had

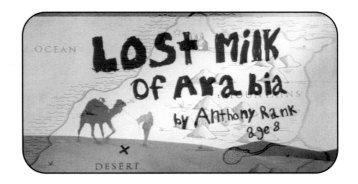

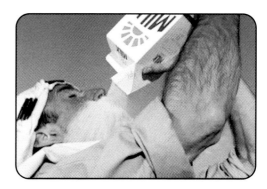

no connection to milk. But scattered among these tailings were some creative gems. The most exciting were dream-like. They were comprehensible. They were definitely about milk, and the loss of milk. But the vocabulary, images, and stories seemed to float, like those from an ancient storyteller (or a modern storyteller in an altered state), and clearly had not come out of the mouths of adults.

"Lost Milk of Arabia"

A perfect example is "Lost Milk of Arabia" by Anthony Rank, age eight. We open on a Lawrence of Arabia type wandering through a vast desert. Camel in tow, he drops to his knees at the appointed spot. Digging furiously, he unearths a treasure box. Ripping it open, he finds a carton of milk and immediately lifts it to his lips. It is, of course, filled with sand. He gags ands spews sand in all directions. A plane, single engine whining, passes overhead, throwing its shadow. The man looks up in angry terror and screams. Moments later our hero enters a bar dominated by a well-dressed colonial with a monkey (a monkey?) on one shoulder and a stunning woman on his arm. "Lawrence" shakes the carton and screeches an accusation. The colonial shrugs, the monkey looks

COMMERCIAL OBSTACLE COURSE

"Lost Milk of Arabia" was shot in the Mojave Desert, with a crew of no less than 50. There were dozens of trucks and enough electrical equipment to power Las Vegas (which wasn't far away). It was ideal. Sand dunes in all directions, a bright but not glaring sun, a great wardrobe, and an excellent "Lawrence." We also had a tribe of incredibly noisy, adversarial dune-buggy riders.

It would take us 20 or 30 minutes to set up a shot. The light and wind were shifting. The crew was exhausted, having established a production beachhead at 5 A.M. The talent was patient, but weary. The cameras, mounted on trucks like gun turrets, needed to be covered from the sand. And we'd get just about ready to shoot when, over the closest dune, would ride five or six guys (of course, guys) on these buggies. The sound was piercing to the point of pain. As if the motors were running without oil, metal on metal. The camel would spook. Our sound man would rip his earphones from his head. "Lawrence" would grab for the reins. The director would curse. And we'd be another half an hour behind schedule.

Options were quickly discussed. Try to reason—a waste of time. Call the authorities—too long a delay. Get physical—my

skyward, and the plane again passes overhead. The spot ends with "GOT MILK?"

The spot started running in January 1998, and kids loved it. We started getting calls and letters from kids (and their parents) offering commercial ideas. Teachers even started using GOT MILK? as a lesson plan to help teach creative writing. While we still didn't agree with DMI's decision to develop special kids' advertising, we had to admit that the work was fresh and fun.

"Return of the Milkman"

No rented camels for this spot (see sidebar). "Return of the Milkman," by Matthew Anderson, age nine, was shot to resemble an old, cheap, black-and-white sci-fi

choice. Thankfully, the buggy riders were more hungry than obstinate. We bribed them with the most glorious buffet lunch the Mojave has ever seen. With that bunch full, fat, and silent, we began to shoot.

We immediately ran into the dreaded "rented camel" problem. One can rent anything in Hollywood. So renting a camel for "Lost Milk of Arabia" was easy. Contact your local animal rental group, provide the specifications, and give them a time and place for delivery. The problem arose because every animal comes with its very own obsessive/compulsive animal trainer. Our trainer seemed to feel that his camel was being asked to do unreasonable things—like walk and stop and walk again. Seriously.

He, the trainer that is, kept calling for camel breaks (and he didn't smoke).

Tensions were escalating to the shoot-out stage when the trainer played his wild card. In the midst of a particularly crucial scene, he called for yet another break. Why? What was wrong now? He proceeded to tell us, and he was deadly serious, that his camel wasn't accustomed to working on hot sand. The director, teeth clenched, pointed out the obvious: that camels evolved over millions of years to work on sand. It was a camel, wasn't it? We hadn't rented an alligator, had we? But the commercial had to have a camel and the only one for miles belonged to Mr. Trainer. We gave up and took a camel break.

movie. It opens on a milk truck spinning out of control and crashing on a lonely mountain road. Years later on a dark, foggy night, we see a mummy-like figure rise from the grave. The milkman has returned. He breaks into a supermarket and carries away two bottles of milk. No soda or juice for our boy. The next day he returns, terrifying the town's populace. He walks into

the same store and asks the fear-struck manager, "Do you give free refills?" We cut to "GOT MILK?"

This spot had everything a kid and client could ask for. Death. Terror. Monsters. Humor. Surprise. All woven into a plot about milk, and all in 30 seconds. Again, kids loved it. Because it didn't preach, didn't lecture, and was written for them by them.

This kids' campaign was insanely simple. It had virtually no boundaries or limitations. It could cover any ground, including what happens to your body when it doesn't get enough milk (you don't want to know). It fed kids' imaginations and their self-esteem. It also fed their appetite for milk. Above all, it put kids in charge. They did the spots; they drank the milk.

The truth was that we didn't really understand many of the spots. They weren't logical. They didn't seem to have plots. Characters appeared out of nowhere. Things happened without cause. When we talked with the young creators, they didn't understand why we didn't understand. The commercials made perfect sense to them. They also made sense to kids in our focus groups. They suggested, none too gently, that we didn't get it because we were *adults.* They used the word as if it were a disease.

Did milk consumption go up among kids? It would be closer to the truth to say that it didn't keep going down. The GOT MILK? kids' campaign helped defend the consumption coveted by Pepsi and Snapple and Gatorade. It also helped establish a stronger, different bond between kids and milk. It was no longer something Mom said you had to drink or "take," but a beverage that kids could talk about, even brag about.

got milk?

chapter 8

Drysville:
The Town Without Milk

On the surface, Drysville was like most small American towns. People woke up, went to work, went to school, went to the local diner for coffee and the local news. But if it was so normal, why did Drysville feel so grim, so gray, so washed out? Why did the residents seem mildly agitated, always a bit distracted?

Was it afflicted with some strange virus? Or run by some rural Mafia?

The answer lie not in what Drysville had but in what it was missing. Drysville didn't have any milk. We didn't know why it was milkless. It didn't matter. Drysville was simply a world of deprivation. A world where everything was not quite right. Where mothers poured tap water on their kids' cereal. Where all the coffee was drunk black. Where cats and kittens went missing.

Why did we create Drysville? What were we thinking, and what did we expect to get out of this imaginary place?

The Drysville story started on a cold, damp day in February 1997. GOT MILK? was just over three years old

The answer lie not in what Drysville had but in what it was missing.

and, by all the usual measures, was performing beautiful-ly. The downward spiral in milk consumption had been stemmed. The campaign was national and winning acco-lades and awards. The licensing program was gaining momentum and generating revenues. The media's infatuation with GOT MILK? was stronger than ever. Hollywood and television were giving GOT MILK? unprecedented levels of exposure. Yet something was askew.

We had just completed another round of focus groups to test several new TV commercial "rough cuts." These were spots that had been produced and edited but not finalized. The sound and music were still sketchy and the color wasn't perfect, but the commercials were complete enough to gauge if consumers understood the story and felt com-pelled to buy and drink milk. The focus groups served another, more subtle purpose: to keep our fingers on the

We wanted to be loved, but not taken for granted.

pulse of GOT MILK? and be sure that the ads were still engaging and entertaining people, that they still looked forward to them, talked about them, and felt personally connected with them.

While the pulse was still strong, it was showing signs of slowing. It was also, for the first time, erratic. It wasn't that people didn't like the work or remember it. Rather, they used words and images that suggest-ed that GOT MILK? had become over-ly familiar. Talking about the new commercials, a teenage boy said they were funny, but he knew where they were going. He was so familiar with milk deprivation and the structure of our commercials that they no longer surprised him. One woman described GOT MILK? as part of her family.

The problem with becoming part of the family was that maybe, just maybe, GOT MILK? was losing some of its leverage, some of its ability to drive milk purchase and consumption. We wanted to be loved, but not taken for granted.

Time for a Change?

Suspicions in hand, I huddled with the Goodby folks. We had old-timers like Jeff Goodby and Jon Steel and a newcomer named Susan Smith. A planner, researcher, and good all-round thinker, Sue had taken the GOT MILK? baton from Steel and was moderating all of our focus groups. As moderator, she was deeply immersed in our culture and was a hypersensitive consumer barometer.

It was a frustrating meeting. Nothing was "wrong." We weren't faced with a crisis. Sales weren't dropping. We weren't in litigation. The board wasn't displeased with the creative. A consumer group wasn't

up in arms. But, like a shadow on an MRI, something wasn't quite right. We needed to bring that shadow into focus before we could recommend spending a million dollars on another round of GOT MILK? TV commercials. You could see people squirming. How do you deal with a creative problem when you don't know if you've got a problem?

We debated doing yet another round of groups. Or maybe a quantitative study (the Linus security blanket of marketing) that would tell us what percent of people liked GOT MILK? and felt it was changing their behavior. In the end, we concluded that the only way to test advertising was to test advertising. We would explore two or three new approaches and see how they stood up to the "classic GOT MILK?" creative.

Before unleashing creative teams, we needed to agree on the parameters of the exploration. Would all the work

How do you deal with a creative problem when you don't know if you've got a problem?

stay true to milk deprivation? No debate. Food and no milk was so relevant to consumers, so much a part of the humor of GOT MILK?, so fundamental to our competitive advantage, that we could not justify abandoning the concept.

Then how about "GOT MILK?" Was this line sacred? Yes! With over 90 percent awareness, it would have taken hundreds of millions of dollars just to get back to where we already were. Further, the words "GOT MILK?" weren't at issue. It was really a question of execution. If the campaign was wearing thin, if it was being taken for granted, the problem was in how GOT MILK? was being expressed and embodied. Ford wouldn't try to transform the Mustang from a hot muscle machine into an economical family car. Nor would they throw away the imagery and equity in the name "Mustang." They would reinforce these assets in whatever design modification they undertook. That's what we were going to explore. Redesigning GOT MILK? while keeping its essence.

But redesigning GOT MILK? was like commissioning plastic surgery on my own child. Every

MORTALITY RATE

Most advertising campaigns are ephemeral, much like mayflies, which emerge, mate, and die within 24 hours. Campaigns often go from inception to production to the creative compost pile within a year, sometimes within a few months. Why, when the average cost of a well-produced TV commercial is around $500,000, would advertisers not stretch the life of each commercial and campaign to its fullest?

The temporal nature of advertising is its greatest weakness. Its transience results from a prism of reasons, some traceable to the shifting marketplace, some to irrelevant and impotent advertising, and some to a lack of continuity, vision, and tenacity on the part of clients, the people who pay the bills.

Changes in the marketplace, shifts in consumer attitudes and behavior, and major assaults by the competition are all reasons frequently given for changing campaigns. Bunk. These are all convenient excuses for advertising that isn't well founded, well focused, and well funded. A truly great campaign is built on a base that is so solid and so broad that, like great companies, brands, music, art, and even cities, it is resilient enough to embrace change. Great campaigns, and the people who manage them, aren't afraid of change—they thrive and capitalize on it.

For example, Absolut vodka has, for well over a decade, used a simple brand name, provocative bottle graphics, and surprising two-word headlines (such as Absolut Brooklyn, Absolut Fashion, Absolut Tarantino) to dominate its category. This enduring campaign has not only encompassed but embraced new product introductions, current events and issues, fashion statements, movies and movie stars, magicians, time periods, dozens of land-

change would be too extreme, every refinement too severe. I was very happy it was Goodby's job to make the incisions.

The Operation Is a Success

We met two weeks later. The creative teams were very excited about their ideas—which only increased my

scapes and destinations, and a multitude of fine artists. Over the years it has prevailed in the face of vicious competitive assaults, an evolution in drinking habits, and massive changes in American politics, demography, and ethnicity. There can be no question that Absolut's advertising has been relevant and effective.

Conversely, much of today's advertising is irrelevant. And irrelevant advertising is always impotent. Irrelevance is inexcusable. It reflects some flaw in the process, an unwillingness to listen to customers, an attitude that precludes other people's ideas. Even the most mundane and boring packaged goods ads, those old-fashioned, side-by-side product demonstrations, were at some base level relevant. Viewers may have yawned and considered going to the bathroom, but at least the message, that Jif peanut butter has more peanuts or Tide gets out the tough dirt, meant something to them, was relevant to their lives.

Clients, the ones who should be demanding lifelong advertising for their products and services, create the most havoc. Through boredom, neglect, or overreaction, they prove lethal to good advertising. It is clients who decide what consumers need to be told and then mandate advertising that fulfills their decision. Changes in upper management have the most toxic effect on advertising. New CEOs, marketing directors, and brand managers all share a craving for their "own" advertising, despite enormous equity in existing campaigns. They literally kill a campaign simply because it belonged to the prior rule. This "capital punishment" seldom makes sense. It is a matter of ego over insight.

nervousness. I was unconvinced that we needed radical surgery, and I knew creative people don't get excited by cosmetic changes.

The best ideas fell into two categories. The first involved a series of stand-up comedy skits by Rowan Atkinson, England's Mr. Bean. Atkinson is a very funny man. He doesn't need to do much to make you laugh. In fact, most of his best comedy is gross understatement. He makes putting on a swimsuit hilarious. Desperation, embarrassment, and guilt are central to his comedy. Perfect for GOT MILK?

Mr. Bean. I liked the Mr. Bean scripts. They were simple, funny, relevant. They used milk deprivation as a springboard but didn't look at all like our classic spots. And GOT MILK? made sense at the end. One script was particularly provocative. The spot opens on Mr. Bean stuffing his face with a brownie and reaching for an unopened quart of milk. As we all have done, he tries to open the wrong side of the paper carton. He struggles for a few seconds before realizing and correcting his error. Unfortunately, his attempts to open the correct side are no more successful. He's losing it and reaches for a screwdriver. Foiled again, he discards the tool and grabs a carving knife. The carton eludes the blade and now Mr. Bean is sizzling, on the

brink of hysteria. Suddenly a demonic grin spreads across his face; he becomes icy calm and leaves the kitchen.

Moments later he returns, a welder's mask over his head, a chain saw in his hands. He fires up the saw and, with utmost glee, shreds the milk carton. We cut away to "GOT MILK?" In the final scene we find Mr. Bean on his knees, attempting to suck milk up off the floor with a turkey baster. There were four Mr. Bean spots, all very clever and very different from classic GOT MILK? commercials.

The second series was built around Drysville, the Town Without Milk. Four great scripts. "Ballad" was the lead script.

Ballad. This ad said, actually sang, it all. The script described a 30-second drive through town. Shot in black and white, the camera moves from a cop looking desperately at a box of doughnuts to a mom pouring tap water on a bowl of cereal. It then passes by a church bake sale with no buyers and a birthday party where the kids refuse to eat the birthday cake. The spot concludes with a pre-teen boy, hormones pumping, paying hard cash to steal a glimpse of a milk pinup. There is no dialog. Only a drawling, bluesy tune with the following lyrics:

Oh Mama oh Papa

I'm feeling so down

How can it be

There's no milk in this town?

Don't give me no baked goods

Until things get better

My corn flakes are cardboard

Cake tastes like a sweater

I'd give anything

For that glass of white silk

I'm living my life

In this town without milk

Clues, Not Answers

We were excited about Mr. Bean and Drysville and immediately put them into focus groups. Back behind the mirror. As is so often the case, research gave us clues, not answers. People liked some of the Mr. Bean ideas, like "Chain Saw Carton," but were unsure who Rowan Atkinson was or if they liked this string bean of an English comedian. It was a moot point. Mr. Atkinson told us he didn't have the time to do the GOT MILK? spots.

Drysville tested well, but not spectacularly. The town without milk concept intrigued and involved people. They wanted to know if Drysville was a real town, who took away the milk, what were their lives like without milk, did the population rebel, were there milk riots?

These groups also reinforced that, at least in California, people were ready for a GOT MILK? refresher course. They loved the campaign but, as we had guessed, were getting almost too familiar and cozy with it. We needed to stir up the dust, get them thinking and guessing again. We recommended Drysville to the board with the understanding that we weren't deserting our core strategy and could return to the classic GOT MILK? approach whenever we wished. They agreed, and Drysville was born.

Commercial #31: Patrol Car

Shooting at night has its own special hazards—like a 25-degree drop in the temperature, gusting westerly winds, a sleepy lighting crew, curious, wandering cows, and bats. Not surprisingly, not much work got done the morning after "Patrol Car" was filmed.

Going Dry

Producing Drysville was intense, complex, and rewarding. Four commercials were filmed over ten days in nine different locations. In one of advertising's great ironies, we shot Drysville, the town without milk, in Sonoma County, California, where there are more Holsteins than people. We literally had to drive dairy cattle off the production set.

Drysville required a director who had the artistic and technical skills to get the look right. One who could work with a broad range of actors, actresses, kids, and dogs (remember, no cats in Drysville). One who could work within a tight budget and time line. And one who could tell a story, our story—life without milk. Jeff Goodby volunteered, and I happily accepted.

We produced three spots in addition to "Ballad." My favorite was literally shot in the dark. "Patrol Car" was aimed at teens and designed to free milk from its "goody, goody," "just for babies" trap. The story involves a carload of Drysville teens who are returning from a milk raid on the adjoining town. These rowdy young men, faces covered in chocolate doughnuts, are on a "milk high." Suddenly they notice flashing lights and are ordered by a highway patrol car to pull off the road. They've been caught in the act. Bootlegging milk into Drysville. The spot ends as the lead cop directs his underling, arms full of milk, to put the "evidence" in the back of the lead cop's car.

Drysville ticked off a number of people. The first call, shortly after "Ballad" began running in October 1997, caught me completely by surprise. A bright, well-spoken woman was concerned about the deleterious effect the commercial might have on homeless people, mothers in particular. She lost me until she pointed out that some homeless people use water on their cereal because they can't afford milk. I apologized and explained that this clearly was not our intent. I also shared that this interpretation had not surfaced in any of our research. She said she understood but still felt that we should pull the commercial off the air. I said we were sorry, but we were confident that "Ballad" was in good taste and was helping to sell milk. "Ballad" would continue to run.

A few people felt it was cruel to show a birthday party where the children had to forego cake because they lacked the milk to wash it down. After "Patrol Car" started running in December 1997, I got

calls expressing outrage that we would suggest driving under the influence, even if it was only the influence of milk.

These folks missed the point. Drysville was a spoof. It made fun of milk deprivation and of itself. It blew everything out of proportion in order to make a point: that milk is absolutely essential to life as we know it. The vast majority of consumers "got it." We were thrilled.

It jolted people out of their GOT MILK? apathy. It wasn't familiar, nor was it predictable. People hummed the ballad and talked about kids bootlegging milk. They recalled the one about a son who drank his way across the country because he couldn't live in a town without milk ("Letter Home," December 1997). And

We needed to stir up **the dust, get** consumers **thinking and** guessing again.

his mom, who after receiving a photo, burst into tears because he was "drinking straight from the carton." People, from little kids to grandparents, liked and understood Drysville.

Moving Beyond Drysville

While the town without milk was a provocative and productive place for us to visit, it wasn't where we wanted to live forever. The reason, which emerged slowly from research, was that the Drysville advertising was working more on people's heads than their mouths and stomachs. People felt the deprivation only intellectually, almost abstractly. Deprivation was happening to "them," the people of Drysville, not to "me," the software engineer in Silicon Valley or the mother of three in Los Angeles.

But tangents are often teachers. We learned from Drysville that the campaign was infinitely pliant. That we could stretch and mold milk deprivation and GOT MILK? to fit a wide variety of eating and drinking situations. That every commercial didn't need to religiously adhere to the food and no milk model. On the basis of this experience, we developed spots like "Paws," a commercial that depicts the terrifying consequences of trying to substitute nondairy creamer for milk. And "Bones," which dramatizes the bodily risk of not drinking milk. We even went so far as to produce a spoof called Y2Kud, a spot in which the power goes out on December 31, 1999, but the cow keeps grazing. But the cow, who clearly doesn't operate

Commercial #42: Peanut Butter Dog

"Peanut Butter Dog" was a work of passion. Two Goodby creative people, Blake and Amy, felt so strongly about this incredibly simple idea that they found a yellow lab, a kid, and a camera and shot the commercial. They added some music, and we had a spot. Total cost . . . next to nothing. Eighteen months later, literally as this book goes to print, we put it on the air, much to the delight of parents, kids, and dogs everywhere.

on microchips, keeps on grazing. There may not be electricity in the year 2,000, but there'll still be milk.

Drysville also reinforced just how important it is to personalize milk deprivation. In Drysville, clusters of people, an entire town, was in need of milk. But we never got up close and personal with any one citizen. In our next few rounds of creative development, we went to the opposite extreme, delving deeply into one character at a time. "Chad," a cocky cooking show host, is incinerated because he doesn't have milk for his hot peppers. In "Hall of Mirrors" an

innocent guy is driven to the breaking point by a clearly visible, but unattainable, carton of milk. And in "Peanut Butter Dog," a young boy runs out of milk and feeds his yellow lab a spoon full of peanut butter. In all three cases, by the end of 30 seconds, we are intimately, irrevocably involved with one character's plight. Our tongues retreat as Chad's mouth is scorched by a searing habanero. We flinch as the poor schlump in "Hall of Mirrors" bangs into yet another milk reflection. And we unconsciously wet our lips as the dog licks his lips, seemingly forever.

Finally, our drive through Drysville demonstrated the value of not just taking, but embracing, intelligent risk. It showed us that we could move off-center for awhile, make some tangible gains, and then return to our advertising roots. As we relentlessly recast and revitalize GOT MILK?, we may even revisit Drysville. Just to remind people that life without milk would be far less tasty and far less fun.

Conclusion: The End of the Tale

Is GOT MILK? the best campaign in history? Probably not, but it doesn't matter. Will it last forever? Certainly not. Despite enormous strategic and aesthetic qualities, advertising is, by its very nature, fragile and transitory. Has GOT MILK? made a difference? Yes, several differences.

Most important, it's made people laugh. There is so much disease, darkness, and disaster in the world that anything that adds a bit of levity is valuable and should be treasured. Laughter lightens us and all those within giggle range.

GOT MILK? changed the world of advertising. It proved, perhaps more convincingly than any other campaign, that advertising can be intelligent, funny, and effective, and that products, even ancient products like milk, can be resurrected with smart, creative advertising.

GOT MILK? also showcased the almost unbounded power of creativity. Today, we are so transfixed by technology we forget that behind every disk and drive, every chip and circuit, was an idea—and an "ideator." Someone who may not have had six years of grad school but who had something more crucial. An open, curious, relentless mind that, working in its own funny way, came up with a huge idea.

I smile every time another GOT MILK? rip-off crosses my desk. Got Hair? Got Bones? Got Teeth? Or perhaps Got Booze? Got Balls? Got Jesus? I smile because these funny, mostly harmless derivations indicate just how deeply and widely GOT MILK? has traveled. It's been an amazing ride. And the ride isn't over yet.

Index

Image Credits